"Robert Staub's *The 7 Acts* (have allowed me to take a more enhance my leadership and personal growth. He affirms that success or failure in life is totally up to me, based on my ability to find and apply courage."

—*Edward M. Gabriel*
United States Ambassador to Morocco

"This book provides the missing piece between knowing in my heart what I need to do and discovering how to do it. I recommend it to anyone ready to discover the next level of meaning in life."

—*Annette Simmons*
Author of Territorial Games *and*
President of Group Process Consulting

"This book is so delightful and easy to read. Through the authentic voice of Dusty Staub come compelling stories, pragmatic tools, courageous inspiration, and centered guidance. Life again sings, and so will you as you read this remarkable book."

—*Jane Penland Hoover*
President and CEO, PenStorkes, and
former President and CEO, Clairmont Oaks

"Every once in a while, a book comes along that touches your soul, moves you, and helps you grow.... You're holding that book in your hands now: It will help you open your heart to exercise greater courage, to view your life's potential, and to fulfill the purpose of your soul."

—*Dave Richards, PhD*
Director, UK product marketing, Nortel

"For those who wish to live a balanced, healthy, and happy life, this results-oriented yet loving book provides a structure for action and a method for finding more fulfilling personal relationships and a more productive work life. It shows that only the individual has the power to initiate changes that ultimately result in lasting happiness."

—*Richard H. Rosenzweig*
Partner, Alcalde & Fay, and former chief of staff,
US Department of Energy (1993–96)

"While others provide 'soup' for the soul, Staub not only succeeds in providing a balanced meal, he supplies the recipe! This work poignantly illustrates the acts of courage required to define who we are and to discover the difference we can make if we put forth the effort to try."

—*Bill Casale*
COO, Echevarria, McCalla, Raymer,
Barrett & Frappier, Attorneys-at-Law

"The *7 Acts of Courage* unfolds into a masterful, self-directed voyage to the center of your being. I personally have used these truths to approach my potential, resulting in greater self-esteem, healing relationships, and a previously unknown appreciation of our power to love and grow."

—*Russ Moon*
COO, Hickory Brands

"In this book, Staub reminds us that to transform ourselves requires self-knowledge and the wisdom to separate the true from the false in ourselves: love from emotion, vulnerability from weakness, joy from sentiment, inner peace from detachment. *The 7 Acts of Courage* accomplishes the crucial work of bringing spiritual values and psychological under-standing into the marketplace of business and daily life. It is a lucid and moving invitation for each of us to live heroic lives distinguished by excellence at every level."

—*Richard Moss, MD*
Author of The "I" That Is "We,"
The Second Miracle, *and* The Black Butterfly

"*The 7 Acts of Courage* definitely brings more heart into the workplace and reminds us that it takes courage to act, to live, to love, and to lead by example."

—*Dan Millman*
Best-selling author of Way of the Peaceful Warrior
and Everyday Enlightenment

"*The 7 Acts of Courage* represents a leap of faith and an opportunity to reconnect to our true selves. Staub's unique approach applies the power of dreams, visions, confrontations, and vulnerability to restore our courage to move and act in decisive, ethical patterns."

—*Lee W. Kinard, Jr, EdD*
Retired news anchor, WFMY-TV (CBS), Greensboro, North Carolina

THE 7 ACTS OF COURAGE

New Edition

BOLD LEADERSHIP FOR A WHOLEHEARTED LIFE

ROBERT E. STAUB II

[signature]

4-18

**Well-Spring Retirement Community
Third Floor Expansion**

The 7 Acts of Courage: Bold Leadership for a Wholehearted Life
New Edition Copyright © 2016 Robert E. Staub II
ISBN: 978-0-9977354-0-6
Printed in the United States of America
15 14 13 12 11 10

Disclaimer: This book is designed to provide information on self-improvement and is sold with the understanding that the author and publisher are not engaged in rendering profession-al counseling or therapy. Those who may be having difficulty dealing with complexities in their personal lives or relation-ships are advised to seek the services of a professional counselor. The author and publisher shall not be liable or responsible for losses or damages caused or alleged to be caused by the use of information in this book. If you do not wish to be bound by this disclaimer, you may return this book to the publisher for a refund.

PUBLISHER'S CATALOGING-IN-PUBLICATION DATA
  Staub, Robert E.
The 7 acts of courage: bold leadership for a wholehearted life / Robert E. Staub II.
Other Titles: Seven acts of courage
  Description: New edition. Oak Ridge, NC: Dynamic Spiral Press, [2016]
ISBN: 978-0-9977354-0-6 (paperback)
ISBN: 978-0-9977354-1-3 (ebook)
  1. Courage. 2. Leadership. 3. Assertiveness (Psychology). 4. Vulnerability
  (Personality trait)
LCC BJ1533.C8   S724 2016   DDC 179/.6--dc23

For permission requests, contact:

Dynamic Spiral Press
PO Box 876
Oak Ridge, NC 27310
Fax: (336) 441–5336
E-mail: *publisher@DynamicSpiralPress.com*
Web: *DynamicSpiralPress.com*

ORDERING INFORMATION

Individual Sales: Dynamic Spiral Press products are available through most bookstores. They can also be ordered directly from Amazon or Dynamic Spiral Press at the address noted.

Quantity Sales: Dynamic Spiral Press products are available at special quantity discounts when purchased in bulk by corporations, associations, libraries, and others, or for college textbook/course adoptions. Please contact Dynamic Spiral Press at *publisher@DynamicSpiralPress.com*.

DEDICATION

This book is dedicated to seven courageous people who inspired and helped shape my life and the lives of many others:

North: Marcie Haynes—Grandmother—who always found the courage to dream.

South: Dr. Martha Carmichael—Mentor and Counselor—who expresses the courage to see current reality with compassion.

East: Leif Diamant—Friend and Advisor—who demonstrates the courage to confront what most of us avoid.

West: Bob Staub—Father, Leader, Patriot—who learned and came to express the courage to be confronted by life.

Up: Dr. Richard Moss—Mentor and Teacher—who walks forward with a resounding "yes" to the acts of courage to learn and grow.

Down: Jeanie Haynes Staub—Mother and Teacher—who expresses the courage to be vulnerable and to love.

Within: Dr. Christine von Clemm Staub—Wife, Healer, Mother of My Children—who always expresses the courage to act regardless of self-doubts or opposition from the powers that be.

CONTENTS

"Be the change you want to see
in the world."

—Mahatma Gandhi

Bringing Spirit to All You Do: Living and Leading Wholeheartedly

For more than thirty years now I have been writing, talking, coaching, and consulting on the need for organizations, communities, families, and individuals to develop the courage to live and lead more wholeheartedly. That theme takes on an increased urgency with the horrific events that have occurred recently around the world. As we move forward, we will need more not less courage, as well as more wholehearted leadership.

All of us, no matter where we live, are challenged to find the courage to not only see the starkness of current reality, but also to have the courage to dream of a better world and act on that dream. As Robert Kennedy so eloquently expressed it, playing off of the words of playwright George Bernard Shaw, "Most see the world as it is and ask why. I see what could be and ask, 'Why not?'"

Our world is rapidly changing its contours and characteristics as we wrestle with the challenges of globalization, the collapse of illusions of safety, and the shrinking of timeliness due to living and working at an accelerated pace. We risk being emotionally and psychologically overwhelmed in the process, diminishing our effectiveness, our capacity to love wholly and live fully. There is the very real danger of losing our resiliency and capacity to bounce back when we encounter great difficulty or have a head-on collision with the unexpected.

Most of us struggle with how to cope amidst rapid change, uncertainty, and threats of violence and fear. If we are to successfully deal with the fear both within and around us, we will need to strengthen our courage muscle. Since the word "courage" is derived from the Latin for "heart," this means finding the means to deepen our connection with our own heart as well as with the hearts of those around us. We need to find the courage to live more wholeheartedly. This means developing our ability to access and use all seven of the acts of courage outlined in this book.

How can you bring a deeper sense of meaning and value to all of your life—family, community, workplace, nation, and world? How can you cultivate the courage to "be" the difference? This slim book offers more than just inspiring stories and examples. It also provides answers and clear practices that can help you to live more courageously while developing person-al mastery and leadership qualities through small, daily acts of courage.

In truth, we all need to learn faster, work more

innovatively, confront more honestly and respectfully, find the courage to be vulnerable, welcome confrontation, and be able to sustain and renew ourselves. Yet it is impossible to do so if we fail to invite and make room for a deeper sense of meaning—for more heart in all aspects of our lives.

The 7 Acts of Courage provides illuminating stories on the efficacy of courage in arenas ranging from the deeply personal to family life to organizations and society. It also offers clear, practical guidelines and exercises to help you develop your courage quotient index (CQI). Take it to heart and you will find yourself living and leading more wholeheartedly. Prepare to be the change you wish to see in the world.

Sing a song of glory, and you'll be that glory;
Naught are you but song, and as you sing you are.

You thought you were the teacher,
and find you are the taught;
You thought you were the seeker,
and find you are the sought.

Sing a song of glory, and you'll be that glory;
Naught are you but song, and as you sing, you are.

—Sufi Chant

INTRODUCTION

The 7 Acts of Courage

I have a series of daring statements I invite you to consider: What you seek is also seeking you. Your life really matters. Who you are and what you are is precious and priceless, and you offer the world gifts it has never had before. You have within you vast potential and unique talents that yearn for expression, and for which the world around you hungers. You also have great power to exert. For example, whenever you change, the world around you also changes. You make a difference by realizing that you are the difference, and that you are needed. This realization places you on the path not only to giving the world what it needs, but to fulfilling your greatest dreams.

Any time we go after what we most want, or pursue something of importance, courage is required. It takes courage to step out of queue and pursue a dream, or reach for your heart's desire. It requires taking risks. It requires letting go of the status quo and striving to create something that different parts of your psyche may doubt. It means facing hardship, ridicule, embarrassment, possibly failure, and, worst of all, your own internal criticism.

Courage is required because to live from the authentic center of who you are, and to pursue or protect what is most precious to you, is not an easy task in our society. Many naysayers, well-meaning colleagues and friends, as well as the fearful inner voices within us, try to keep us in line. We are challenged to keep quiet, conform, and step back into preassigned roles and ways of behaving. We are assailed by inner doubts and fears, sometimes by threats, but most often by misunderstanding and puzzlement, or by the not-so-subtle judgments of those who don't understand what we are doing or who may be threatened by our increasing authenticity.

During the past 30 years, I have had the privilege of working as a consultant with many successful executives and business owners, as well as their families. What I have seen has been both inspiring and heartbreaking. These people have accomplished much to be proud of, but many suffer from constricting belief systems, overworked bodies and minds, neglected families, aching hearts, and spiritual hunger. Many are living as if their lives don't matter.

I also have had the opportunity to work with less "successful" members of our society: handicapped children, underprivileged families, financially strapped workers, and people on welfare. The sacrifice and personal triumph they often demonstrate is encouraging, yet the same pain can also be seen in their lives. These two diverse groups yearn for a more vital experience of being alive, feeling valued, and believing they make a difference.

My experience is that most of us are simply overwhelmed by change and the incessant demands of the workplace, our families, and the society around us. Our senses are constantly assaulted as multiple entities jockey for our attention, time, and commitment. It becomes difficult to navigate the encroaching demands of each day and keep a firm grasp on our souls—remembering to nurture and nourish the core of who we are. We are drawn to the periphery of life and we live from that edge rather than from the center. In the process, we lose our way. We are out of touch with the vital core of our souls. As one executive put it, "I feel as if I have no self. All I do is struggle to meet the needs of my boss, the workplace, my children, and my aging parents. There's nothing left for me—or of me—by the time I fall into bed."

But there is a better way to live—a pathway to the center of heart and life. It is not far away. In fact, what you most desire is very close, but it may be difficult to take the steps to get there. To find the path and walk it requires daily acts of courage.

The Path of Heart

What is courage? Where does it come from? How can you cultivate it and bring it into your personal and professional life?

The word "courage" comes from the French word "*coeur*," which means "heart." Courage, then, comes from the heart and must return to it consistently for guidance and renewal. Thus informed, your daily exercise of small acts of power prepares you for life's larger challenges. Practicing courage is to remember the essential truths confirmed by a deep inner sense: that your life is precious, that you matter, and that you have gifts that the world needs.

Courage is not to be found in one great heroic act, but in day-to-day actions that spring from the center of who you are and from your willingness to take the path of heart. This means to call forth your deepest aspirations, act based on what you believe is right, and persist in the face of fear and in spite of the intimidation you may receive from others or feel inside yourself.

To own and direct your life in all its dimensions requires the conscious and intelligent exercise of courage—demonstrating heart. Even more significantly, it often inspires—and taps into the motivation of—others, who then follow your initiative. Thus you become a leader to those around you, including your family, friends, and co-workers, as they become aware of your vision and integrity when you engage in daily acts of courage.

Even if you do not see yourself as a leader, the presence of courage (or the lack of it) in your life makes a great difference in how you experience yourself and how you move through the day. For example, if we lack the courage to hear how we may have hurt someone we love, we do not listen to what they say; we damage their trust, their love, and thus, the relationship. Or, if we lack the courage to tell the truth about what we feel or think, we do not express ourselves and end up feeling alienated or diminished. If we lack the courage to pursue our dreams, we end up with lower self-respect and a gnawing sense of inadequacy. If we lack the courage to reach out for the relationships we most desire, we end up with remorse and regret.

I am convinced that courage is desperately needed if we are to live lives of purpose, meaning, love, and fulfillment. Courage today is in short supply. The failure to find courage has led to an increasingly fragmented society filled with divisive personal and institutional agendas. Our political leaders, for the most part, demonstrate a penchant for expediency—the "quick fix"—and lack the courage to tell the truth to the electorate. Many industrial leaders have also failed to model courage, seeking the lowest common denominator and the easiest answers when faced with the toughest questions and challenges in our rapidly evolving "information revolution." Displaying candor and facing tough choices require courage, and accessing it could make great leaders of these same people if they—if we—would exercise it.

In Western society at the minimum, we too often lack the courage to face the truth about how we have been living and the decisions we have been making or avoiding. It is time to wake up and face the current realities. We must somehow find within ourselves the heart to open our eyes and look beyond our expectations, hopes, fears, and past beliefs if we are to gaze unflinchingly upon what stands before us, and what we must do.

The 7 Acts

What if the deepest part of your heart could find a more fulfilling and loving connection with life? What if you could live your life with greater awareness of how precious, valuable, and important life is? What if you could direct your life from the center of who you are toward the realization of all you can do and all you can be?

Through the exercise and cultivation of acts of courage, you can start living your life today as if all aspects of who you are really matter—creating a deeper, richer connection to your heart and to the hearts of those around you. Each day then contributes to a deeper and more satisfying sense of purpose, vitality, and aliveness whereby you grow stronger in your capacity to exercise love, enjoyment, and power in your life.

I have identified seven distinct acts of courage needed to create the lives we most desire and live from that place of greater authenticity. These acts encompass the whole of who we are and who we can be. The seven acts of courage are:

1. The courage to dream and put forth that dream.
2. The courage to see current reality.
3. The courage to confront.
4. The courage to be confronted.
5. The courage to learn and grow.
6. The courage to be vulnerable, to love.
7. The courage to act.

These acts of courage work on different aspects of our psychological, emotional, spiritual being. They strengthen and refine the connections between our internal world and the external. These acts help us develop increasing levels of personal power, efficacy, and ability. Each one strengthens our capacity to relate meaningfully to every moment while building our ability to create more effective and loving relationships with others. The acts of courage connect us to our higher selves—to the dimension of the spirit—and open us up to more constant communion with God.

At this point you don't need proficiency in all of the acts to achieve success or create a more joyful life. Simply learning which act to call forth and practicing it allows you to function at higher levels anywhere, with anyone and at any time. In fact, I recommend that you work to build your courage quotient index (CQI) one act at a time. Each time you engage with courage, even if it's only a small act, you build capacity for your next, perhaps larger, act of courage and this expands the power and authenticity of your self-expression as you expand your CQI.

Use this list to help you become more powerful and effective. For example, select the acts of courage you have no difficulty with—the ones you practice easily and often. You can build on these strengths and give yourself encouragement to step up and out even more. Then consider the form or forms of courage you don't often practice—those you avoid or simply haven't worked on. Begin today to consciously cultivate your CQI through practicing the underused acts. By focusing on these and using the guidelines in the following chapters, you can significantly increase your personal power, effectiveness, and satisfaction in life.

Ask yourself which act of courage you most need to practice on a day-by-day basis. What situations are you currently facing that could be transformed by acting with an expanded CQI? What have you been avoiding that you most need to face, and which act of courage will be most helpful in dealing with it? The seven acts can help you diagnose and prescribe—for individuals, couples, leaders, teams, and organizations—a new framework for dialogue, under-standing, and mutual focus.

Why are there seven acts? Why not just two, or three? It

turns out it takes at least that many to capture the fullness, range, and depth of the courageous actions required for a "wholehearted" life. In fact, the number seven plays a powerful role in our lives and psyches every day: There are seven days in each week. Historically, the number seven has been a symbol of wholeness and religiously—a sacred number since ancient times. We are impacted by seven-year cycles. Our bodies regenerate themselves every seven years. There are seven major directions for earth based cultures: north, south, east, west, up, down, and within. Seven, then, signifies completion. Certainly we can think of other acts of courage by narrowing and focusing the list provided, or by using different words to describe similar things. But I feel the seven acts described in this book encompass the courage that lead most effectively to the living most fully and even to the completion of the soul.

The Law of Correspondence

As you build courage and prepare to take the next steps in going after what you really want in life, you can apply the "Law of Correspondence." This at its simplest says that an image or metaphor for your goal can be used in a literal sense to prepare you for a larger action. The image "corresponds" with the action you need to take. So, by beginning with small actions that correspond to your goal, you are prepared to take much larger steps. In fact, these smaller, "practice" acts of courage often move you farther down the path toward your heart's desire than if you had taken larger steps without being prepared.

The ancient foundation of this law is found in the statement, "As below, so above." A story that captures the power of this principle comes from an executive (let's call him Bill) I coached at a Fortune 200 company. He and a colleague thought they were in the running to succeed their long-serving boss when he retired. Instead, the CEO brought in someone from outside the industry and new to the organization. The whole department was in shock, as this was not the usual practice. Promotions most often took place from within the ranks.

The new head of the department was a command-and-control, "take names and kick tail" kind of executive. He basically told his direct reports, "Just do as I say and follow my lead in all matters." This did not go over well, to say the least. There was resentment, frustration, and a sense that the team members were being devalued. Complaining in the hallways, after meetings, and between staff members skyrocketed. In addition, in meetings, the new senior manager talked while the others simply listened, and sullenly participated offering minimal input. A dark and anxious mood permeated the department ranks.

Bill wanted to break free of the emotional shackles constricting him and his ability to contribute more to the work process and organization. He knew that to do so, he would need a more courageous way of engaging with his boss. Yet he lacked the courage. He was afraid of being put down, embarrassed, or put on his boss's shit list. He was stuck.

We came up with the idea for him to try something new to express himself more fully, that would challenge him and require courage. Bill told me he had always wanted to sing, but had been told he could not carry a tune in a bucket. He felt self-conscious and embarrassed at the thought of singing in front of others. The fear of doing so, however, was not as great as speaking more directly and honestly with his boss. Bill was willing to step out and work on his courage quotient by engaging in something that was anxiety-provoking but within his range of willingness.

Bill signed up for voice lessons with a singing coach. She was able to help him rediscover the part of him that loved singing when he was a boy. With her help, he was able to not only carry a tune, but also put emotion into the tone of the words he expressed. After a few months of practice— once every two weeks with the voice coach—he was not only singing in the shower, but also as he drove to and from work. The next step in building his CQI was to visit a karaoke bar, sign up for a song, and sing to those present.

Bill reported that he was terrified as he stepped up to the mike, yet he was determined to follow through. His prior practice helped. Though he started off with a shaky voice, he steadied out and at the end was belting out the old Elvis standard "Fools Rush In." He got mixed applause, but what really mattered was realizing he could go beyond old self-doubts and fears to do something he really wished to do—a breakthrough.

Over the next month, Bill sang two more times at an open karaoke mike and felt his confidence grow. In a follow-up coaching session he told me, "Now I am ready. I am not as afraid of speaking up and engaging my boss. I am still anxious, but I know I can do more than I have let myself do in the past." We worked on his strategy and approach to having a more courageous conversation and way of working with his boss now that he felt he could "sing" in a new tune and more authentic voice than before.

Within the next week, Bill approached his boss asking for a meeting to discuss how he could better support the work process. His boss initially brushed him off, but Bill persisted, asking three powerful questions I had suggested:

1. What is the one thing I am doing now that best supports your vision for this department?

2. What is the one thing I need to change or do differently if I am to be of the most value in realizing your goals for this department?

3. What is the one thing I can do to help make you even more successful?

The meeting that resulted led to an in-depth discussion—the first ever—with his supervisor. Bill took notes, asked follow-up questions, and then, in a week, came back with an action plan asking for further input or refinements. In the coming months, Bill reported feeling valued, more engaged, and that his supervisor was not only asking for his ideas, but actually acting on some of them.

Bill's success was a direct result of developing his CQI by practicing something that corresponded to the key thing he needed to do: "speak in a more authentic and courageous voice" and "step out and do something desired yet feared." By bite-sizing it—bringing it down to a less threatening set of actions—Bill was able to build his quotient of courage and take the difficult step of engaging his intimidating and challenging boss.

If there is something you would like to do, but your fear or self-doubts hold you back, find an image or metaphor that reflects what you want to do. Play with the image; find a way to physically embody it and practice doing what you want at a symbolic level. It might be "stepping out," "revealing yourself," "hanging out a shingle," "turning off" old behaviors, or "embracing" a new way of being. Whatever the image may be for you, use it as a means of exercising and developing your CQI to prepare yourself for the larger act of courage to create what you most deeply desire.

The Law of Correspondence lets you know that you

don't need to have all the courage right now. Instead, you can develop what you need over a period of days, or even months, as you safely practice with a living image or metaphor of the action you want to take.

Another example of this capacity to build your CQI:

A wealthy, high-powered executive I worked with realized one day that he had been so busy building his career and developing his company that he had become a stranger to his family. He had lost his center, working 80 hours per week. His health and his family were damaged. He wanted to develop a more intimate and loving relationship with his eleven-year-old son, especially since his wife and he were separated and he only had visitation rights a few times a week.

"It's too late for my marriage, but I hope it's not too late for my son and me," he said. Yet when he was with his son, he found himself constricted, anxious, uncomfortable, and awkward. He was afraid to take the relationship to a deeper level and he felt pained to discover that he didn't know how to talk to his son in a meaningful way. His son had become a stranger to him—an angry, demanding, and difficult stranger at that.

I asked him to find an image that would correspond with what he wanted to create with his son. He struggled with this for a few minutes and then said, "Look, all I want is to feel that my son and I are walking together, in synch, as we share some exciting adventures." I encouraged him to take that image of walking together as the key to creating a new relationship with his son.

Soon they began to take walks along some of the old canals in town, simply discovering the waterways. As they walked, the father not only found physical relaxation, but he soon found himself tentatively and awkwardly moving into emotional discovery and revelation. He shared his regrets with his son about what he had missed out on with the family. By the fifth walk, his son began to soften his angry tone and share, with tears, how much he had missed him. The boy also began to talk about himself and what a stupid, no-good person he thought he was. His father, appalled at the boy's self-image, shared how proud he was of his son as well as his love for him. The boy opened up and told his father that he thought something must be wrong with him since his father never spent time with him. Both father and son ended up in tears during this conversation.

Over the next four months, the image of walking together helped both father and son grow in their capacity for greater acts of courage, allowing them to reveal deeper emotions and discover new dimensions of themselves in the process. During their many walking adventures, the father developed the courage to be vulnerable and found greater intimacy with himself and his son as a result. The boy also developed the courage to confront and to be confronted and was able to share his self-doubts with a loving and attentive father who could help. As the two began to draw closer to each other, they were not only able to strengthen their relationship, but they began to heal their respective "heart" conditions as well.

Each chapter in this book focuses on one act of courage, helping you understand how the different acts work on various parts of your soul and spirit. The chapters will serve to develop your capacity to access and exercise each specific act of courage. At the end of each chapter is a summary, along with exercises designed to make the concepts come alive in your life. Although you may already be practiced in some of the acts of courage, the exercises will help you attend to and strengthen them on a more conscious level. Keep in mind that the acts you do not yet practice are the ones holding the keys to unlocking your potential and living your life more joyfully and wholeheartedly.

SUMMARY AND EXERCISES
Using the Law of Correspondence

First: Resolve today to begin to live your life in a whole-hearted way, knowing that each act of courage really matters. Begin by thinking about what is most important to you. Write down your answers to the following seven questions:

1. What do you most deeply desire?

2. What is most precious in your life?

3. What forms the center of your life experience?

4. If you could live and experience your life as you truly want, what would you do differently? How would you feel?

5. What are the deepest guiding values and principles by which you seek to live?

6. If you could change your life for the better—so that you were living from what is deepest and best in you—what would you change?

7. What would that change do for you in terms of living from your heart?

Second: Resolve to begin to find and create the courage to live from your center, honoring the depth and richness of your heart. Look for opportunities to exercise "daily acts of courage."

- Start by asking yourself what you would like to do but are afraid to try.

- Find a corresponding image or metaphor that captures the essence of what you want to do. Some examples include: "taking a leap," "walking in harmony," "spending time on discovery and exploration," "embracing something new," "turning over a new leaf," and "dancing to a new tune." Find something that speaks to your heart.

- Once you have found a corresponding picture or symbol, create a means for engaging it in a daily activity. For example, if you have chosen the image of "dancing to a new tune," find a new song or form of music you have never danced to, and then dance to it. Dance privately at first, and then look for opportunities to dance with others. The act of dancing to a new tune will begin the process of learning something new while helping to make the larger change. When you risk the embarrassment of not getting the steps right with the new tune, you are exercising courage and pre-paring yourself for the larger act of courage that will follow. In the meantime, you are taking steps toward having a greater CQI and the capacity to move forward with more grace and confidence.

Introduction

"Sing a song of glory..."

THE FIRST ACT

THE COURAGE TO DREAM AND PUT FORTH THAT DREAM

The courage to dream and put forth your dream is essential if you are to claim the power to create your life and bring out the best in yourself and others. It is the first act of courage because it provides a context for all the others. It allows you to orient yourself at any time and in any place based on a consistent vision that forms the inner core of your amazing strength. This act allows you to pursue what you most desire, pulling you toward a more powerful sense of self and self-worth.

This act of courage requires simply that you claim all you aspire to be. What is your dream, your deepest desire? What do you hold most dear? What would you bring to life if you could? What is the "song of glory" you wish to sing?

What does it mean to "sing a song of glory"? Remember, if you can, Martin Luther King Jr's "I Have a Dream" speech. Dr. King developed and refined his dream over many years and gave voice to his "song of glory"—his dream of a nation undivided by prejudice and hatred. Many listened and took courageous steps toward greater racial equality and harmony as a result. But the song is not finished and did not die with him. The song lives on, touching and inspiring others with its power and affirmation. People continue to sing that song of freedom and equality. His courage to dream and put forth that dream has been a great gift for us all.

What Is Your Song?

Perhaps your "song of glory" is to be a loving parent, ensuring that your children grow up healthy and whole, confident in their self-worth and knowing how much they are loved. Or maybe it is to create a new business, or a product or service, providing meaningful employment for others. Or it may be to write a book, direct a film, or teach a course, reaching out to touch the hearts and minds of many. Whatever your "song of glory" is, you must first find the courage to articulate the lyrics and then "sing the song."

This song comes from deep within your heart. To sing it requires your full capacity to tap the tremendous power of imagination, create images that capture your deepest longing, and then communicate them. You can tap into and formulate symbols that reflect your highest aspirations and greatest desires, all coming together in an integrated rhythm you can move to and from which you can create. This is the beat of your song.

To identify your song and then sing it requires the courage to appear naive, challenge your self-limiting beliefs, defy your circumstances, and face the judgments, criticisms, and cynicisms of others. If you do not cultivate this primary act of courage, you risk missing out. You may leave your greatest gifts and talents—that could otherwise enrich and edify others—undeveloped. You will lack orientation—the context for guiding and directing your actions and those of others around you. You will wonder why life seems dull and meaningless. In fact, you may miss out on singing the very song you came here to sing, instead being left standing silent before the vast mystery of life, or merely playing your part in the cacophony around you. You leave your life in the hands of chance and the decisions of others.

On the other hand, to practice the courage to dream and put forth your dream is to say:

"I can envision a better tomorrow; my imagination is source of power, and my dreams matter."

It may help to remember the line from Proverbs, "Without a vision the people perish."

The courage to dream and put forth that dream requires that you formulate a vision for your life. You must craft your dream, refining it through each major challenge you face. Then it requires communicating your vision—whether in a relationship, a team, at work, or in the community—and engaging others in its creation. As you live your dream, clarifying and articulating it as you go, you give voice to your own unique "song of glory."

Intention and Attention

This act of courage comes first since it sets the tone and direction, and establishes meaning, for the other six Acts of Courage, providing a foundation for your life. It works at the soul level through two simple mechanisms: First, your dream or vision activates the power of intention—what you truly wish could be. Second, putting forth your dream then activates, in your day-to-day behavior, the power of attention—what you focus on and what continually draws you toward the accomplishment of your intention.

Intention is the power of choosing an internal compass and reference point. It guides the way you live your life and defines, as you interact with people and situations, what you wish to create—not only in your life, but also in any project, work group, or enterprise in which you are involved. Intention is the creative purpose that informs and directs all you do, both in your personal life as well as your career. It provides coherence, meaning, and purpose to all your activities. For example, if one part of your dream is to create a loving, nurturing relationship with your family, then your "intention" is to love and let yourself be loved, to nurture and be nurtured. This intention provides a context for all interactions with your family.

Richard Moss, author of *The Second Miracle: Intimacy, Spirituality, and Conscious Relation-ships*, uses the word "consecration" when asking people what they intend to do with their lives. By this he means: What are you making sacred, or giving your life over to? What matters most? What is the aim of your life? What drives you? Consecration is your deepest intention—the lodestar that provides orientation and direction.

Attention, on the other hand, is the power of focusing your consciousness and life energy in the present. This power gives traction to your vision and supplies the means of manifesting what you intend. Using the example above, it is not enough simply to intend to love others and be loved by them. Intention is only the first step. The next step is to express that intention in your words and actions by paying attention to how you respond to family members and others. Attention means noticing what works—as well as what doesn't work—and what then gets in the way of creating what you intend.

Attention is the practice of being mindful, of noticing what is going on, while observing your behavior. Attention then provides clues to behaviors that are off purpose with what you intend and to which you are blind. It clarifies what works and what doesn't work in making your dreams reality.

The Courage to Put Forth Your Dream

Before our marriage, my wife Christine and I sat down and wrote out our "dreams" for our life together. Then we carefully questioned each other and made comments as we elaborated a vision statement. We defined and clarified what we wanted both from each other as well as the union itself. This exercise formed both the individual and joint intentions for our lifelong commitment to each other. It took several days of soul-searching and conversation. The second, and much harder, part was to remain conscious of, and attend to, the different ways our words and actions supported our intentions.

One evening, a few weeks after we had drafted our vision, we found ourselves arguing. She had called me "stupid" and then pretended nothing happened. I became upset, provoked by all the self-doubt I carried and the hurt I felt over the many times that word had been said to me growing up. But instead of sharing my pain, I became self-righteous and, in a lecturing tone, said, "I certainly don't call you names. It is unloving and not in keeping with our vision for this relationship for you to do so." But instead of seeing the error of her ways and apologizing, Christine simply withdrew and refused to talk with me. So, out of pain and fear, I upped the ante. "Well, maybe we should simply forget the wedding!" Then I stormed off. She came after me with a vengeance, angry and hurt.

As I looked at her face, I saw the effect of my words and actions and realized, with a shock, how much I had hurt her. I paid attention to her pain and remembered what I had intended to create in my relationship with her. I felt ashamed and apologized. "I blew it," I said. "You deserve much better than the way I've been acting. I'm sorry."

She took my hands and we looked at each other, seeing the pain and the longing we both carried—not the defensiveness and self-righteousness perfected in the years before we met. We restated our dreams and reminded each other of our intentions for our relationship. The pull of our dreams— our combined vision—was compelling. We then talked through our conflict, learning from each other and deepening our understandings about old wounds and defenses. And because we had the courage to view our argument in the context of our collective vision, we arrived at a deeper level of intimacy.

It takes courage to admit to yourself the truth of what you want to be and wish to create. It often requires deep soul-searching, exploring the beliefs, fears, and judgments that block you from clearly formulating and articulating your dreams. It also takes courage to put your dreams forward, to remember them in the day-to-day struggles, to restate them and shift their context to a higher purpose. Often it takes the courage to risk feeling embarrassed or awkward.

A highly successful senior executive that I had been

asked to coach had just been reprimanded by her boss. As she fumed, she glared at me. "How dare they do this to me! I've done everything for them! Everything! I don't deserve this kind of treatment. It's the work of a disaffected few, poisoning the well. I won't stand for it!"

She was beside herself with fury and rage. Yet I also saw, at a deeper level, hurt and shock. As I listened, I wondered how such a competent and committed executive could be so blindsided by her own staff, whom she cared deeply about. Later, as she calmed down, she stopped pacing and sat at her desk. In a plaintive tone, with her head in her hands, she asked, "What did I do wrong?"

She continued, "My staff is afraid of me. They say I treat them with contempt!" She went on to explain how she had worked to make them successful and how proud she was of their accomplishments—that is, until her boss came to her with their complaints.

She was a no-nonsense, results-focused manager. She drove herself and her people hard toward ambitious goals and high standards. Those who worked for her both respected and feared her. She was quick to criticize what she viewed as performance-endangering behaviors. Because excellence was expected, it was never praised. She was passionate about success but, as one team member put it, "It's like she's on a mission from God, but no one is clear about how we fit into that mission. Only one thing is certain: Nothing had better get in her way!"

As we talked, I discovered this executive cared deeply about each team member's success. I asked her to outline what her intentions had been. She created a list that was very positive: "For each person to soar, to be seen as value-added, to be seen as a high performer, to be promotable, for the team to have fun doing great work." It was a great list. I then asked if she have ever shared it with her teammates. She said, "I have always believed actions speak louder than words. My team should know my intentions by how I challenge them." She really didn't like the "touchy-feely" stuff and felt awkward about discussing anything other than quotas, tasks, and goals. She held back praise because she felt embarrassed, and she didn't want to appear idealistic or naive by expressing an impossible-sounding vision. She was stunned and hurt to discover her behavior had created the opposite of her intentions.

This executive had gotten herself into trouble by not exercising the first act of courage. The fear of being embarrassed stopped her and she assumed the team would simply know her intentions and feelings. She lacked the courage to articulate her dream and they lacked context for her actions. Instead, she left her staff to fill in the blanks, which meant they interpreted her behavior from their anxious perspective. They had not understood what she was striving for, or how they fit into her plans. The only organizing force was her personality, the goals she set, and her corrective feedback. She had failed to call forth their aspirations and provide a reason for them to take risks with her. And ultimately, her staff saw no way to resolve festering team conflicts and problems.

Over the next few hours, we discussed the team's perceptions and how they were created. We discussed her tactics as a manager and her conscious and unconscious behaviors in dealing with her staff. Then we charted an intervention to help her begin the change process. The executive and her team went on to create a shared vision and strategy for working together. Her connections and effectiveness as a leader expanded the team became a powerhouse of excellence in the organization. Members were sought out by other departments because of their ability to articulate a dream and work together to achieve it.

The power of exercising the courage to dream, of actually singing your "song of glory," is awesome. It clarifies and defines your intentions. Then it becomes the guiding star on which to focus your attention and the attention of others. It boldly expresses your heart's aim.

SUMMARY AND EXERCISES
Developing the Courage to Dream
And Put Forth That Dream

"Sing a song of glory..."

The courage to dream and put forth your dream is essential to creating and living your life with greater authenticity, effectiveness, and personal power. It forms the backbone of a consistent and loving sense of direction and orientation, allowing you to direct your attention in all that you do so you can manifest your intentions. It forms the creative center of a joyful and fulfilling life.

First: Unleash the power of conscious intention. Take time right now to reflect on where you want to go and what you wish to accomplish. What is the "dream" for your life? What do you intend to experience, create, do, be?

Exercise:
Unleashing the Power of Imagery to Create Your Dream.

Gather a stack of different magazines and newspapers and cut out the pictures that appeal to you or to which you are drawn. As you search for images, keep asking yourself: "What is the dream for my life? How would I like to experience and create my life?" After you have selected the ones you like best, take a large piece of paper or cardboard (16" X 18" is a good size) and arrange them into a collage. For added effect, you may also select things you can touch—both visual and kinesthetic.

- List your goals and aspirations. What is the under-
lying theme running through your list? Summarize it
in two sentences. Notice how you feel about them.

- Arrange the two sentences into a vision statement
that speaks to your heart. Make sure it's what you
really want, whether or not you believe you can make
it happen. Ensure the statement captures how you
would like to experience your life and relate to others,
as well as what you would like to achieve. Notice the
feelings your statement evokes.

- Read your vision statement out loud in front of a
mirror, looking into your eyes as much as possible.
Notice your feelings and observe any doubts. Believe
in the importance of the vision, even if your mind
says it can't be realized.

- Consciously choose your vision. Say, "I choose
this vision. I choose to believe in it, in spite of any
doubts."

- Find someone who cares about you and whom you
trust to share the vision statement with. Ask for their
support and encouragement.

Second: Unleash the power of conscious attention. Help
make your dream a reality by focusing on it and bringing the
power of attention to bear on what you are doing, what is
going on around you, and how your behaviors work to serve
you or work against what you most aspire to do and be.

- Write your vision statement on several 3" x 5" cards. Post them in highly visible places such as your refrigerator, car visor, bathroom mirror, desk, next to your computer screen, or on the inside of your planner. Carry a copy in your pocket or purse, or use one as a bookmark.

- First thing in the morning, occasionally during the day, and the last thing at night, look at your vision statement and repeat it to yourself out loud. Remind yourself about what you most desire and about your aspirations.

- Find opportunities to talk about your vision and your commitment to it with people you trust and who care about you.

- Observe your interactions with others and notice what works to draw you closer to your vision—as well as what doesn't. Consider what you do, whether habitually or reactively, that may be working against the realization of your vision.

Third: Harness the synergy of intention and attention in all you do. Now that you have created and fine-tuned your dream, you must actively cultivate the courage to create secondary, or functional, dreams in your major life activities. These secondary dreams serve to reinforce and move you toward the realization of your life vision. It is your "song of glory" and you are working to make it a living reality.

- List the major activities going on in your life. For example, one executive listed the following: parenting, leading a work team, heading up a major project, coaching his daughter's soccer team, dealing with a dying parent, and maintaining his marriage.

- For each of the activities, starting with the most significant, write out the outcome you wish to create. Specify your intentions on paper. These form the secondary dreams or visions that support your overall life vision.

- Condense these secondary statements into one or two sentences at most.

- Write out a brief statement about how all your secondary dreams reinforce and support your overall dream.

- Revise your statements based on what you see and feel. Make sure each of your dreams interlock in your mind and reinforce what you most deeply desire to experience and create in your life.

- Sit down with important people in your life and share your secondary vision for your interactions with them. Let them react. Ask them for their thoughts and feelings.

- Invite them to create with you a unified set of intentions, along with some guidelines on how to help each other focus attention on the realization of these goals.

The Courage to Dream and Put Forth That Dream

"...and you'll be that glory."

THE SECOND ACT

THE COURAGE TO SEE CURRENT REALITY

If the first act of courage—to dream and put forth that dream—is the foundation for creating your life in a meaningful and powerful way, then the second act—the courage to see current reality—is the ground upon which that foundation stands. It is the willingness to listen to and notice the current song of your life: How are you singing it and experiencing it? What results are you creating? What are you expressing? How are you feeling? What is working and not working? What have you made of your life so far?

It takes great courage to see current reality—and see it clearly—without using the great defenses of the ego such as pretense, excuse, denial, blame, or rationalization. Your current reality includes not only the things you are proud of and all your accomplishments, but also the things of which you are ashamed, or that you would rather forget or just won't see. This includes your defeats and losses. For most of us, it is easy to justify or deny our culpability in problematic relationships, troubled work environments, or disappointments in life. It is hard to see and own the places where our living experience is painful, constrained, or diminished. It is difficult to accept criticism. These painful experiences are the sum of our losses, disappointments, and self-doubts. They indicate where we have abandoned our power by giving in to fear or self-limiting beliefs.

It is a powerful step to take when we assume 100% responsibility for our lives and our behaviors. Courage is required to do so, to look at current reality, especially the parts we don't wish to see and have skillfully avoided. When we do not take stock of present reality nor assume responsibility for it, we dupe ourselves and make it difficult, if not impossible, to correct behaviors that undermine our intentions.

Why is the courage to face current reality so essential? And if it is so important, why is it number two on the list? Why not make it number one?

It is essential to see and understand where you stand in the world—to observe what is working and not working for you. If you do not know the current reality and take responsibility for how things really are, you have no accurate reckoning or basis for moving forward. You have no place from which to push, no ground to provide traction as you go about making your dream a reality. Yet, without the courage to dream and put forth that dream, you have nothing to move toward. Looking only at current reality leads to one of two dangerous reactions: If your current reality is comfortable, it means complacency. If it is painful or difficult, it generates cynicism, anger or despair.

In 1956, my father was assigned to command the U.S. Army base in Stiffkey, England. During the transfer of command, he was asked to sign a form certifying that the goods listed on the inventory for the base were present and accounted for and that he accepted responsibility for them. This included weapons, munitions, fuel, and vehicles in the motor pool, etc.

Usually in such transfers, the incoming commander conducted a simple walk-through inspection and then verified with the previous commander that all was in order. But Dad, at that time a captain and taking charge of his first base, was nervous and had a penchant for detail. So, rather than a walk-through inspection, he under-took an extensive personal inspection of every major item on the inventory list to satisfy himself that all was in order. The departing base commander, a major, could not leave or relinquish command until the inspection was completed and the form signed. Since he outranked my father, he ordered him to cease the inspection and sign. Dad respectfully declined. The major became angry, accusing him of holding up his departure, but my father insisted that he needed to complete his inspection.

At the end of the inspection, my father told the major he could not sign the form because some significant inventory items were missing. The major then called the commanding general and complained that this insubordinate young officer was holding up his departure and calling him a liar—after all, the major had already told my father all the goods were on the base.

Dad was in agony about what to do—he wanted desperately to take over the base and did not want to rock the boat. He just wanted to sign the form and get it over with, but he could not do so in good conscience. Seeing no other alternative, he began a recount.

At this point, the commanding general paid my father a visit and inquired "what in the hell" he was doing delaying the major's departure and holding up the administration of the entire base. My father explained that he simply couldn't account for over a quarter million dollars' worth of inventory that the manifest said should be there. At this, the general lost his temper and called my dad some names that would probably scorch this page if I were to repeat them. Then he ordered my father to sign the form and be done with it.

Dad, trying to stop the trembling in his hands and legs, took the pen from the general. In that moment, he faced two dreadful options: sign or refuse to sign the form. He could sign the form—he rationalized—the goods were probably on the base somewhere. Someone had simply messed up the inventory. Things like this were known to happen all the time and maybe he was being too rigid. Additionally, he reasoned, he now faced a direct order. On the other hand, he could not account for the discrepancy and would be out of integrity to sign something he could not verify. However, if he did what he thought was right then he risked severe reprimand. His career might go up in flames—and he had a wife and three young children to support.

He leaned forward to sign the paper, feeling relieved but, at the same time, cowardly. He put the pen to the line for his signature and then paused. The pause lengthened. The general cleared his throat and said, "Captain, just sign the damned thing. Do it now!"

Then my father laid the pen down, stood at attention, and said, "Sir, I cannot sign it." Though he felt terrified, he also felt he had just won a major victory.

The general glared at him and asked, "Captain, are you refusing to obey a direct order? Think about your career. It's hanging in the balance." "Sir," my father said, "I can not obey an order which requires that I falsify a report to the Army. You may very well wreck my career for this, but sir, you have no right to order me to lie or misrepresent the truth. I am liable for what I sign. If I sign this, I am stating that the manifest is correct and all the items are on the base. Sir, more than a quarter million dollars of goods cannot be accounted for. They are missing. I will not lie, nor will I sign for what is not there." My father was terrified, but he clearly saw current reality. In spite of his fear and his desire to please his superior officers, he stood by what he knew in that moment to be correct.

After a long pause, the general signed the form in his own name, saying, "Captain, you will live to regret defying me." Then he said, "Assume command of the base. The major is relieved." Dad returned the salute and left the room on rubbery legs.

Later, my father found out there had been an ongoing theft ring operating at the base. Not only had my father made the ethical choice, but he also had been wise. His ability to see current reality not only protected him in that instance, it ultimately furthered his career. To see reality—in spite of what everyone wants you to see—is a daunting task. We face great pressure to conform to established norms. Often we are ridiculed, threatened, shamed, or punished for defying conventional viewpoints. It takes great courage to step back and honestly assess current reality. For want of doing so, many people in all walks of life have failed themselves and their enterprises.

Once I was called in to consult with a manufacturing company. The president seemed open and eager to make his organization function at a higher level. I asked him to tell me about the company's business plan and strategy. He had a clear vision of what the organization needed to do and a well-thought-out plan. He had acted on the first act of courage: daring to dream and putting forth the dream in a strategic plan.

Next we assessed the company's current reality. When

asked about how the company functioned, especially at the senior management level, he acknowledged a few problems, but nothing serious. He explained that he empowered his associates, letting them manage themselves. He also mentioned that the company was owned by two brothers who made their fortunes by buying up, leveraging, and growing inexpensive companies. The president reported to them quarterly, but the brothers had left him virtually alone to manage the business. "They are strictly hands-off," he said.

Then I interviewed each of the president's direct reports on the executive team. Each one described an organization with great strengths that currently faced a severe crisis. The senior executives, all competent and bright individuals, saw themselves as a dysfunctional team. The company's margins had begun to erode. Manufacturing problems were cropping up and quality was now an issue. Each described the conflicts faced by management, but declared that the president seemed unwilling or unable to help them function more effectively.

The executive team met weekly to discuss operations. The meetings started at eight in the morning and often ran late into the day, frequently involving open shouting matches and long, drawn-out arguments. At the end of the meetings, the group typically broke up with no clear agreement or action plans. Everyone hated the meetings. The consensus was that during each twelve-hour session, the team only accomplished about 45 minutes of real work.

When I next met with the president, I asked him what he expected to hear about the company's strengths and weaknesses. He accurately described the strengths, but struggled a bit with the weaknesses. He had a clear view of the organization's challenges, but he was vague about the executive team's problems and showed little insight into his own role in it all. I asked some probing questions, but he was unable to articulate anything else.

I asked the president if he was open to hearing some unpleasant information from his team which, if he failed to address, would impair his progress toward making the organization more productive. His smile never wavered and he said, "I've never been afraid to hear the truth, even when it's only the opinions of others."

At that moment, a little red light went off in my head about his readiness for the information. Since I felt he might not be ready to handle the team's feedback, we discussed the importance of perception and how it governs human behavior. Then I presented my summary.

The company faced three major challenges, "The first involves the satisfaction of your key customers." He nodded his head in agreement. "The second has to do with your direct reports and their collective dysfunction as a team."

He stopped smiling and remarked, "I think 'dysfunction'

is too strong a word. I believe they're a good team; they just need a little fine-tuning."

Carefully and respectfully I responded, "I understand you are proud of their abilities and you see them as a team. They want to become a functional team, but they do not currently feel they are one." He took out his pen and wrote a few lines on his notepad. Then he looked up, nodded, and asked, "Okay, what's the third challenge?"

I suspected that the president would have the most difficulty with the third point, but he needed to hear it. "The third opportunity involves your leadership and how to make it more powerful and effective." I elaborated, "Your direct reports appreciate your delegating to them, your belief in empowerment, and your patience in letting them work things out on their own. You are also an encouraging coach. But that is also the challenge you face in leading the team. Since the team is not operating well, they need you to step out of the coaching role and become a director—a more hands on leader. At the moment, your coaching style is working against the needs of the team. Right now, they need intervention, direction and mediation."

The president's jaw clenched, he put down his pen and looked out the window. "Thank you for your report. I'll think it over and give you a call." I tried to catch his eye, but he refused to look at me.

"Sir," I said, "I would like to give you more substance and

help you think through the best course of action." But he was quite adamant about the session being finished. He stood up and extended his hand. I knew, with a sinking sensation, that he was in deep denial. He wasn't going to look at the current reality for his team or himself.

I took his hand and said, "Thank you for your time. Please consider what I've said. I know from experience that the owners you mentioned will not stay 'hands off' if the executive team continues to function as it has been and you do not address the challenges." Without a word, he sat down, picked up the phone, and dialed, dismissing me completely.

Nine months later I was informed the owners had fired the president and all but one of the senior executives. The president had refused to see current reality. He failed himself, his team, the owners, and the whole company. Instead of dealing with the reality his team faced, he acted according to what was most habitual and comfortable, crashing both his career and the business into the hard reality of non-performance.

Why do so many intelligent people miss the obvious, focusing on what they wish to be true versus what is currently true and staring them in the face? The answer lies in how our minds distort reality to protect us from doubts or protect our cherished assumptions and beliefs. Many of us simply do not wish to see something that indicates we might have to change our lives and way of doing things. Current reality can be inconvenient and downright unpleasant. It often challenges conventional wisdom. Courageously facing current reality means we may upset people who are unwilling to see it and they will, in turn, pressure us to back down or subscribe to their viewpoint.

In the short term, not looking at current reality—whether in a relationship, your career, your business, or your own life—may protect you from pain. But in the long term, if you do not cultivate the courage to see current reality, you set yourself up for much greater pain and failure.

We all have powerful psychological defenses we use to blind ourselves from seeing current reality. It takes courage to challenge these defenses and see beyond them. They include:

- Denial
- Repression
- Projection and Distortion
- Rationalization

Denial

Refusing to see what is in front of us is called "denial." When faced with information that contradicts our view of reality, we refuse to acknowledge it. Sometimes we do not even notice it is there at all, blinded by our prevailing mind-set and viewpoints. We do not allow ourselves to entertain or recognize any other perspective or alternative.

As in the case of the president in the story, denial allows unpleasant facts to simply disappear. This is the "see no evil" monkey with its hands clamped firmly over its eyes, blocking any viewpoints that may threaten or challenge current behaviors.

Denial, carried too far, destroys careers, relationships, and even your health. We can easily recognize when someone close to us is refusing to see current reality. The challenge is to recognize when we are doing the same. It takes courage to see past denial because it means we will have to change something in our lives or in the way we think.

Repression

The capacity to block out and "forget" painful experiences is a coping mechanism. However, repression of painful memories also means we can end up blocking out the insights and lessons we might learn from those experiences. This then limits our ability to see reality, especially when it resembles or reminds us of prior painful experiences. We push the memory out of our minds to avoid pain and preserve the status quo. It takes courage, then, to see beyond repression because it means we will have to deal with whatever pain may still be there.

Years ago, when I had a clinical practice, a young mother of two sought my help. She suffered from severe panic attacks involving heart palpitations, nausea, and vertigo and was convinced she was going to die. She had been hospitalized multiple times. The attacks had become so bad that she refused to go anywhere unless her mother could take her.

Over the course of six sessions, she made some progress using different techniques to control panic: breathing slowly and consciously from her diaphragm, focusing and shifting her internal self-talk, using mental rehearsal, and learning various calming methods. But the real breakthrough came when she worked up the courage to stop repressing her anger and frustration with her husband. She had been taught "good girls don't get angry," so she concealed her feelings from her family. But when she could claim her anger and speak out for what she really wanted and needed, her anxiety completely disappeared. She became a powerhouse in her family and community. Her husband was delighted with the change— only now she was more challenging and demanding of him!

Projection and Distortion

This mechanism allows us to shape and re-interpret reality, hearing and seeing what we believe to be true regardless of what we face. In a literal sense, we distort what is in front of us and see a projected image or preconceived idea. We experience our fears, doubts, wishes, hopes, expectations, beliefs, and ideals instead of what is really there in order to make the situation or person fit into our beliefs, prejudices, and feelings.

A common projection occurs when we meet someone

and immediately like or dislike them. Something about them reminds us of someone else, so we "project" onto them that same internal image and react accordingly.

When I initially met my first partner in business, Kirtland Peterson, we were working in another consulting firm. I immediately didn't like him, seeing him as arrogant, cold, and judgmental. But, understanding something about projection, I was suspicious of my first impression and made an effort to work with him in order to get below the surface. As we worked together I found him to be humane, sensitive, and delightful. Later, after our friendship had grown, I shared with him my first impressions. He laughed and told me he had felt the same way about me at first.

The power of projection and distortion is that we do not think to check or challenge them. They "feel" right and are largely unconscious, automatic responses. But to live our lives as if they really matter—to create joy, love, and long-term success—we need to find the courage to challenge these automatic patterns; to review our version of reality and see the truth.

Rationalization

This, for many, is the champion of psychological defenses, the one most common and heavily favored. Everyone makes use of it—perhaps several times a day. Rationalization explains away any evidence that doesn't fit your viewpoint or self-definition, talking yourself out of dealing with unpleasant reality or facing some painful issue. It is also a way of justifying something we want to do but know to be wrong. For example, some people rationalize padding a travel expense account, explaining to themselves that the company "owes" them for all the travel they have to do. Or they reason that the company can afford it since it is only a small amount of money. Besides, the extra means much more to them and they "deserve" it, anyway. Such rationalizations are used to make peace with their actions.

These defenses are some of the ways we block ourselves from seeing current reality. It takes courage to plow through them and clear away the protections we put up to preserve our illusions and make ourselves more comfortable. Yet, without a clear view of current reality, we are flying blind— at the mercy of circumstances we do not see, unable to take them into account in our planning, thinking, and actions. We end up without a foundation to reach for our dreams.

SUMMARY AND EXERCISES
Developing the Courage to See Current Reality

"...and you'll be that glory"

Your ability to hear the "songs" being sung in your life, and to know your current way of "singing" with the impact you have on those around you, is imperative in creating a deep, rich life of love, joy, and success. It means cultivating the second act of courage—seeing current reality. To do so requires the willingness to challenge your automatic ways of thinking, feeling, judging, and perceiving. Are you willing to see what is so, even when those around you have a vested interest in not seeing it and are invested in pressuring you to accept their own perception of reality? You foster this act of courage if you:

First: Resolve today to begin to live your life informed and aware of the reality around you. Establish a foundation from which to move toward your dream by honestly assessing your current reality.

Remember the powerful psychological defense mechanisms that can block your ability to see current reality. Check for the ways you employ these mechanisms: denial, repression, projection and distortion, and rationalization.

Make a detailed inventory of the way you feel about your life, considering all aspects. Take the next 20 minutes to write your answers to the following questions, noticing the ones to which you are drawn—and also the ones you feel like avoiding:

- What do you most resist hearing or get most upset about when people give you feedback about: Yourself? Your work? The way you live or behave?

- How is your family and home life?

- How is your work life?

- How are your friendships?

- How is your relationship with nature and the world around you?

- How is your health?

- How do you feel about yourself?

- How is your emotional life?

- What forms the center of your daily life? Is it fulfilling, or less fulfilling, than you would like?

- If you could live and experience your life as you truly wanted, what would you be doing differently? How would you feel? (Contrast this to how you are currently living.)

- How is your career? What are the business and market realities you face?

- How are your finances, and how do you feel about them?

- What do you feel in your heart?

Second: Resolve to begin to live from your center, honoring the truth by stating your current reality—both the pleasant and unpleasant aspects. Resolve to tell the truth about the quality and experience of your life, noticing where you tend to avoid what is unpleasant.

Look for opportunities to exercise this act of courage by telling the clear, unvarnished, and unabashed truth about who you are, how you feel, what is going on, and where you stand.

- Start by noticing what you most often find yourself resisting and arguing about. Entertain the possibility that you are defending yourself against a deeper awareness. Take the courageous step to explore the viewpoint you most resist and ex-amine it for any truth you may have missed.

- Ask someone you trust to help you take a detailed and honest look at how you act, react, and impact others, and how you come across when dealing with others.

- Write down your current reality by de-scribing it from both factual and emotional points of view and describe how this reality impacts others. Tell the truth with compassion and gentleness. Find someone to share that reality with and let them counsel you.

- Interview the key people in your life, personally and professionally. Ask each of them: What are the top 3 things I am doing that I should continue doing, and why? What are the 1 or 2 things I need to stop doing, and why? What are two things I need to start doing and why? And/Or consider asking for a 360 feedback process to be used to gather feedback from your supervisor, peers and any direct reports regarding your strengths, top two opportunities for improvement and the best advice offered. Then look at the themes around strengths as something upon which to build and the themes around areas for development as your challenge to grow.

"Naught are you but song..."

THE THIRD ACT

THE COURAGE TO CONFRONT

A fundamental truth I have discovered in my work and life is the axiom, "When you avoid confronting something today, you create a bigger problem tomorrow." Whenever we back away from confronting a difficult issue, it doesn't disappear or get better on its own. It festers, grows, and undermines our power. When we avoid confronting painful situations or problems in relationships, we inflict damage on our souls and compromise our integrity.

The courage to confront—the third act of your CQI (courage quotient index)—is how you "sing." We are shaped as much by what we confront as by what we avoid. Confrontation provides the leverage by which we can move from current reality toward our dream. First, you must develop the courage to dream—to know where you want to go, outline your intentions, and focus your attention. Second, you need the courage to see current reality, to know the foundation from which you start. Third, you must have the courage to confront if you are to move forward from the base of current reality towards the "dream." The courage to confront is essential to your power to express yourself and find your true "voice." It frees your spirit and allows you to express the fullness of who you are.

A corollary to the axiom is "Pain is inevitable." We may deal with a small issue today and feel a small amount of pain, or we may deal with a greater issue and face greater pain later. When we avoid confronting a problem, it doesn't disappear or go away. Instead, its impact on us grows, the potential pain grows, a pattern unfolds, and, when the inevitable moment of reckoning comes, the pain is ten times worse as a result of our avoidance.

Imagine that you are going to ultimately have to swallow something, let's say a toad. Now, would you rather swallow it when it is a tadpole or after it has grown into a 10 pound toad? Or, as the great philosopher on dealing with things, Barney Fife of the Andy Griffith show would express it: "Nip it in the bud!"

A colleague recently told me about the deaths of two of his neighbors that occurred in the space of three months. The first was a 37-year-old man who was rushed to the hospital one afternoon with severe chest pains. The doctors told his wife that her husband had suffered a heart attack. From his hospital bed, the man confided he had been feeling chest pains for the past several months, but failed to confront the problem. Instead, he had rationalized away the pain. Within days, he was dead. His wife was left to raise their two young children and face a burden of grief and bitterness toward her husband for having been so "thoughtless" in not confronting the pain sooner, or even sharing his problem with her.

The second man, in his early 40s and who had been a friend of the first man, witnessed the suffering of the first family. He and his wife extended support to the first man's wife and their two children. Yet, within a few months, he also died from a heart attack, having denied his own chest pains for weeks. He was unable to learn from the tragic mistake of his friend. He also lacked the courage to confront his pain and the potential situation he faced.

Not all failures to confront situations or people end so tragically. However, I have seen all too many marriages and partnerships break apart due to the failure to confront painful problems early on. This also applies to failures in careers, teams, and organizations. When we don't confront important issues, they compound and grow until the moment of reckoning arrives, bringing even greater pain and unpleasant con-sequences than it otherwise would have.

What is so difficult about speaking your truth? What is so daunting about addressing a challenging problem or opportunity? Most of us fear that:

- We will have to change or do things differently.
- We will experience pain, rejection, loneliness, or retaliation.

- We will hurt someone else or damage an important relationship.

- We will be "wrong," embarrassed, or humiliated.

During the first few years of marriage, I noticed that many times whenever Christine was upset with me, I had a way of making it her fault—justifying myself by making her wrong. Developing more of the courage to see current reality, I began to see a dark and largely unconscious behavior at work. It was part of an emotional defense developed in childhood to protect self-esteem when I felt attacked or belittled by my parents, teachers, or the new children I met as the Army moved us from place to place each year.

Although I had the courage to see what was going on, I lacked the courage to confront it or share it with my wife. I was afraid she would reject me or take advantage of me if I shared the problem with her. Yet, my acts of self-defense, denial, and blame drove us farther apart, eroding our relationship. I practiced telling the truth to myself, confronting the situation in my mind by writing in my journal and reminding myself of what I most deeply valued and wished to experience. It took over a year of such preparation—and of experiencing frustrating and ultimately unsatisfying encounters—before I could confront the problem, in the moment, and with integrity.

One Saturday, Christine had just finished confronting me about the mess in the house and the lack of help in dealing with it. At first, automatic defenses kicked in, telling her how tired and frustrated I felt about having to work so hard to provide for the family. I began to point out her shortcomings and all the things she wasn't doing. Predictably, she became even more upset. Suddenly, a neon sign seemed to light up in front of me that said, "Moment of Truth: She's right!" I felt terror, then guilt, and finally deep remorse and sadness.

Gathering my courage, I stepped back and sat down. I looked past her angry face and saw the frustration and hurt. Taking a deep breath, I confronted the situation.

"Sweetheart, you're right. I do make you wrong and end up justifying myself. I'm sorry." She looked surprised and suspicious. I continued. "This is a pattern I've had for many years and I am ashamed of it. You don't get a fair hearing and this is not a loving way of relating to you and your concerns. I am stuck and need help in breaking this pattern. You deserve better and I want better for us."

We then had a breakthrough conversation in which we both confronted the ways we tended to blame each other. What began as a "fight" soon became an emotional sharing and discovery process.

I have both participated in as well as seen the pain and damage caused when people avoid confronting problems with themselves and others, not only in the personal arena, but in the professional world as well. For example, an executive with whom I worked, was asked by his boss, the president and CEO of the company, to confront an employee who was causing problems with a key customer. But the executive hated confrontations; they were messy and could spin out of control. He had little practice in, and almost no stomach for, confronting people. He knew the employee had the technical skills to satisfy the customer. He also knew the employee could be a royal pain, often coming across as arrogant or sarcastic.

The executive had been avoiding a confrontation, even though members of his team complained about the employee in the past. Using an old friend, the psychological mechanism of rationalization, he figured the employee's behavior would not be an issue for long, since his technical abilities and results would eventually outshine his problematic people skills. He also believed that if he gently "suggested" that the employee use more tact with the customer, the employee would "get it" and modify his behavior. Finally he sent an e-mail to the employee, reminding him of the importance of treating the customer well and including some tips on how to help others feel valued and suggesting the employee work on interpersonal skills.

One month later, the executive was again invited to meet with the president. As he walked into the president's office, he was surprised to see the director of human resources sitting in the office. The president inquired about the employee and asked the executive what he had done to address the problem. At first, the executive spoke in generalities, but the president pressed him for specifics: "Did you call him in for a face-to-face conversation? Did you write him up? Did you ask him for a specific and measurable improvement plan?" Finally, the executive candidly explained that he had sent the employee an e-mail and some suggestions.

The president sat back and asked the director of human resources to speak. The director handed him a memo and asked him to read it. The message was a written warning, charging the executive with endangering the financial well-being of the company. It warned that disciplinary action would follow if he allowed one of his direct reports to alienate an account due to poor professionalism or training.

The executive pleaded, "But I did take action! I warned him in my e-mail. It was his failure, not mine!" The president responded, "Your actions were wholly inadequate for addressing the serious behavioral issues of your employee, and you have not followed through on the directive I gave you. You did not confront the issue nor the person effectively. An e-mail is not the same as a face-to-face discussion. Also, you did not make sure the employee had a development plan to improve how he interacts with others, or address the concerns and complaints of the customer."

The executive was speechless. He knew the president was right, but he could not concede it. His mind raced through several rationalizations and justifications. After a long silence, he asked the president, "Do you want my resignation?"

The president responded, "No. I want you to learn from this experience how to become a more effective manager. In the meantime, this has shaken my confidence in you and it will take you some time and effort to rebuild my trust."

The executive then took an important step. "I need some help in learning to effectively confront problems with people. Will you assist me with that?" Both the president and the director of human resources agreed to his request. With coaching support the executive gradually learned to confront others more effectively.

The courage to confront requires you to deal with what is in front of you, to tell your truth with compassion. To do so requires the courage to challenge your automatic ways of thinking, feeling, and perceiving. It also means speaking out about the truth as you see it. My close friend, associate and co-author of another book, Wayne Gerber, is a good example of this. Wayne's father, a rabbi, had always said that Wayne must marry someone within the faith.

Then Wayne met Debra. The relationship had depth and a power he had never felt before. Unfortunately, Debra wasn't Jewish. So, after realizing he really loved her, Wayne asked her to convert. She thought about it for a while, but decided it wasn't right for her. Finally he asked Debra to marry him and she said yes. He knew he would have to confront his father in order to claim the life he wished to have with Debra. It was one of the most difficult things he had ever done. He had always held his father in high esteem, always seeking his approval, but he was sure of instant rejection.

Wayne told his father he had decided to marry Debra and that he hoped his parents would accept her and his decision. His father became upset and Wayne received the rejection he anticipated. But he persisted in facing his father and telling him what his relationship with Debra was about. His father withdrew and Wayne began to plan for the marriage, unsure of whether he had lost his father's love.

Finally, the wedding was set. Wayne's father refused to come. Debra and Wayne found another rabbi to conduct the service. At the last minute, Wayne's father decided to attend. During the ceremony, the rabbi conducting the service called Wayne's father to come forward and say the blessing over the couple. He did so, and father, son, and daughter-in-law embraced.

Sometimes, as with Wayne and his father, a confrontation can lead to a breech in a relation-ship. Yet, if what we are called to do, if what we are reaching for, requires the courage to confront, then we must either confront or step away from our heart's dream.

Which creates the greater harm: Confronting those we love with something we believe they will reject or disapprove, or denying our deepest desires? Ultimately, if we are to make our dreams reality, we must develop the courage to confront.

One more fundamental truth can be found in confrontation: When we have the courage to con-front, we also create an opportunity to take our relationship to a deeper level. Though confrontation can be traumatic and stressful, it can lead to greater connection and understanding. For example, Wayne's relationship with his father deepened as Wayne found the courage to assert himself and claim the life he wished to live. The act of challenging his father's judgment forced both Wayne and his father to view their relationship from a different perspective. The pain led to a deeper dialogue and ultimately, a heartfelt connection that enriched their lives.

The courage to confront is the courage to sing the song you were meant to sing. Yet that song reveals itself only as we learn to express our viewpoints and ourselves on life. Learning to confront small situations—when the stakes are not high—prepares you to confront larger issues and deal with confrontation successfully when the stakes are high.

SUMMARY AND EXERCISES
Developing the Courage to Confront

"Naught are you but song..."

The ability to "sing the song" you were meant to sing depends on accessing the courage to confront problems and compassionately speak your truth. To do so requires the strength to challenge automatic ways of thinking, feeling, and perceiving.

How to cultivate the courage to confront? Start with reminding yourself what life is really about. Review core values and aspirations—dreams. Ask yourself what you want to experience: a greater sense of aliveness, or a sense of diminishment? Then look at the current reality. What in life do you need to confront? What has been avoided? Write down what you wish to create and outline the people and situations that have to be confronted to make dreams a reality.

Here are some other additional things that can be done to create this act of courage and develop your capacity to "sing out."

First: Resolve to speak the truth with compassion and claim the life you wish to live.

- Ask: What do I avoid speaking about when I am with someone that I later wish I had said?
- What do you most wish to experience in life? What are your feelings about yourself? How best express life?

- Make a list of the times you have failed to confront an issue, situation, or person. Write down the feeling states it engendered and what the consequences of not confronting were. Notice the price paid for not confronting.

- List three current people or issues you would like to confront. Describe the benefits to be experienced by confronting with compassion.

Second: Imagine yourself successfully confronting someone you love.

- Mentally rehearse one of the confrontations—pick one you feel most positive about being able to deal with. Imagine yourself in the situation, saying the crucial words with authority and compassion. Notice the positive feelings that come with doing this.

- Repeat the mental rehearsal two more times, imagining the words, the way your body would feel, how you would sound. Imagine being successful.

- Now do the same for the other two situations. Feel your innate ability to confront expanding in power and scope.

- Rehearse one more time, focusing on speaking with respect and compassion.

Third: Resolve to confront, with tact and respect, the situation or person you feel would be most ready (and able) to hear you.

- Notice how you feel and what happened. What tone was used? Were you able to hold your truth and yet remain compassionate? Rehearse doing it even better and congratulate yourself for having confronted someone or something that needed to be addressed.

- Look for opportunities to exercise your courage to confront in day-to-day life.

- Take small steps. Gently stretch yourself each time, always using compassion and respect.

"…and as you sing, you are."

THE FOURTH ACT

THE COURAGE TO BE CONFRONTED

Learning from criticism is what the fourth act of courage is all about. Instead of viewing the world as a source of threat, we can turn difficult situations into opportunities to become more effective and powerful. Not reacting to criticism as an attack, we can appreciate our critics as teachers who have important lessons for us. The courage to be confronted opens doors to incredible learning and greater personal power.

The courage to be confronted is more than just the flip side of the courage to confront. This form of emotional strength is critical to true integrity. Without the fourth act of courage, it is easy to end up off course and out of balance. Once you have developed the courage to formulate your dream, exercised the courage to see current reality, and cultivated the courage to confront, you are halfway home. The fourth act—the courage to be confronted—is where you develop and exercise even deeper integrity by demonstrating to others your commitment to live and act from your center, from the heart of who you are creating yourself to be. This form of courage allows you to learn from the insights, criticisms, and challenges of others while enabling you to make necessary course corrections.

This act of courage is rare—few of us have it nor have we seen it modeled effectively. We are constantly on the alert for criticism, prepared to respond to it decisively. Yet our very agility in our self-defense suggests that, by definition, we will learn only slowly and haltingly. We vigorously defend our points of view, patterns of behaving, and ways of relating to the world. This prevents us from living our lives more fully. We become slow learners and increase the chances of being blindsided.

When we were young, our parents modeled for us how to give and receive criticism. Now we live and interact in a society that reflects those examples. Consider what we have been given: Whenever we are criticized (translate: "attacked"), generally we either resist and defend or launch an attack. Occasionally we retreat, but this tactic is more often an avoidance strategy rather than a helpful tool. We see these behaviors in our homes, offices, in public, and in social interactions. This way of dealing with criticism and feedback is hideously flawed; it doesn't work. It creates greater pain and suffering while preventing or seriously inhibiting our ability to learn and grow.

Most of us have been hurt by the words and criticisms of others when we were vulnerable, consequently building emotional barriers to protect us from criticism. These barriers cause us to go on automatic defense whenever we feel someone is either critical of us or of something we have done. It takes courage to step out from behind our protective shields and really listen to what is being said.

But it is not enough to confront others—we must also allow others to confront us. In fact, inviting feedback regarding our impact on others and opening ourselves to criticism and ego blows makes us stronger and more aware. We become much more effective when we are willing to become students again and learn from others. The willingness to be taught by the criticisms, suggestions, and confrontations of others is an essential act of courage.

The successful playwright Neil Simon once told a radio audience about a time when one of his plays opened off Broadway. He knew something was wrong with the second act, but he just couldn't figure out what it was or how to solve the problem. A local theater critic wrote a scathing review of the play after seeing it. Simon called the critic, who, when Simon identified himself, responded defensively. But Simon shocked him by asking him out to dinner. Over dinner, the playwright asked for more of the critic's observations and scribbled furiously into his notebook as the critic laid out all his thoughts and criticisms. Simon thanked him and paid for his meal. Then, using the man's critique, he rewrote the second act and fine-tuned the first and third acts. The play went on to gain great success and critical acclaim.

If Simon had lacked the courage to be confronted—to actively seek out criticism—he would not have been able to grow and improve. In fact, by asking for more information about what the critic disliked, he was able to make his work more powerful and effective.

In Defense of Defenselessness

I have another proposition for you: The only real defense is defenselessness. The most powerful and intelligent thing you can do when you feel criticized is set aside the impulse to defend yourself. Instead, vigorously pursue the critic's line of thought and point of view. Seek to understand the context in which the person sees you or your words and actions. Explore the person's feelings, thoughts, and ideas. Look for the truth of what they are saying. Then ask yourself: What possibilities are here for me to become more effective? What can I learn about how I have been thinking and behaving? What does this person need from me in order to give me the best they have to give? What would be the most effective thing to do? What can I learn from this criticism? How can I best respond to this criticism to have the impact I want to have?

Defenselessness opens doors, creating possibilities you would have otherwise missed and allowing you to grow in influence with the other person. On the other hand, what does acting defensively get us? It creates resistance and resentment from those who have the courage to confront us. We merely confirm for them that we are exactly as they see us and communicate that we are not willing or able to hear them. This leaves us more vulnerable, more exposed, and less informed. Being defensive, we open ourselves to error and the possibility of failure.

Most of the time, we send out strong verbal and nonverbal messages to others that say, "Don't confront me; cater to my ego." We deflect the information that would allow us to learn quickly and interact with others more gracefully and effectively. In our automatic, well-rehearsed, and largely unconscious defenses, we create greater pain and suffering for ourselves and remain blind to the consequences.

According to an article in the *Wall Street Journal*, many people believe it is unwise to be completely honest with their boss. If we are asked to give an honest, candid evaluation of our boss's strengths and weaknesses, we generally deflect or tell a white lie. After all, the ego is a fragile thing, and the ego of a boss is particularly fragile. And if we are completely honest and open, we will likely be punished later on. Therefore it should come as no surprise that most executives are dismayed by what those who work for them say about their strengths and weaknesses when that feedback is supplied anonymously. The fact that they are caught by surprise and have to struggle to digest the information is revealing in itself. It forms an indictment of our models for handling criticism and confrontation: Because of how we process criticism, we have become learning impaired. Therefore our management and leadership abilities are likely to show only a slight improvement over time.

But it is not only in our corporate offices that the courage to be confronted is lacking. As a marriage and family therapist, I saw many individuals, couples, and families damaged by their unwillingness to be confronted, or even hear the criticisms, from those they loved and who loved them. I saw firsthand the damage and pain these defensive patterns created.

A family once came to me for help in dealing with their "troubled" 16-year-old daughter. Mother and father were at their wits' end and the family—the three of them, plus another child —was in constant turmoil. The girl, whom I'll call Sally, was angry, hostile, and verbally abusive, and had recently been suspended from school for fighting. Her parents, Elizabeth and Jim, outlined her problem behaviors and described how they had dealt with her. When I asked Sally what she thought, she glared at me and wouldn't speak. Elizabeth tried to prod her, but Sally remained silent. Jim appeared angry, yet I saw redness around his eyes and sensed a great sadness. He sat with folded arms, watching his wife.

After several sessions of observation and interaction a deeper insight emerged. During our third time together, I asked Elizabeth if I could say something to Sally. She nodded, never taking her eyes off her daughter.

"Sally, you seem to have a lot bottled up inside of you. I want you to listen carefully to what I will say. No one has ever said anything like this to you before. Are you ready?"

The teenager turned and looked at me for the first time. She appeared curious and a bit suspicious, but after a moment of silence, she nodded.

"Sally, I think it's very brave of you to try to protect your parents. You are working very hard at it, and you must be exhausted."

Her eyes opened wide and she began to cry. Her parents stared at me: Jim with surprise, and Elizabeth with what appeared to be shock. Sally, wiping her eyes, sobbed. "It must be very hard for you to take so much upon yourself, but I think it's time you let your parents take care of themselves. You need to take care of Sally—you have really neglected her. You must feel lonely, sad, and angry about all this."

Sally nodded, her whole face softened, and the anger seemed to melt from her body. Her father saw the change and a faint smile formed at the corner of his mouth, but Elizabeth continued to look shocked.

I asked Jim to tell me what my words had meant to him. He looked first at me, and then at his confused wife. Finally he found the courage to speak up. "It just makes sense. I think you were telling her that she isn't responsible for the problems between me and my wife."

Elizabeth in confusion asked him, "What are you talking about? This is about Sally, not us!"

Jim replied, "No, I think it's about you and me. Sally has been caught in the middle."

His wife turned to me and started to say something but her daughter interrupted. "Mama, I'm sorry to have been so difficult. But I have been very mad at you and Papa. You are unhappy and it is very painful to watch." Sally cried as she said these words. Her mother's mouth dropped open, speechless. I spoke up, "It was evident from your interactions that you have a great deal of tension in your marriage. Jim seems defeated and sad. Elizabeth, you seem frustrated and unhappy. Sally has been acting out the anger and frustration between the two of you in addition to working out the challenges of adolescence. She has served as the glue to hold you together, but the burden is now too heavy for her. You both need to face the problems and challenges in your marriage, and Sally needs to take care of herself."

Jim sighed. "Elizabeth, I can hear the truth in what he's saying. Can you?"

Elizabeth looked at him as her tears began to flow, "I wasn't aware you were so unhappy with me!"

"I think it's more that you are unhappy with me," he replied. "That's what I have felt, and because of it, I have withdrawn and closed down."

This breakthrough eventually led to a revitalized marriage for the couple and a much more rewarding life for Sally and her brother. The hardest part was helping Elizabeth get to the point where she could hear the pain of those who loved her. She had blocked out her husband's complaints and the criticisms of her daughter, becoming the "power broker" in the family. As long as she would not hear what others had to say, all that was left for them was to withdraw and shut down—like Jim—or rebel—like Sally. But as soon as Elizabeth made it safe for them to speak up without punishing them for their opinions—the marriage and family life improved dramatically.

In the process of defending ourselves from confrontations, we deny the perceptions of others and do violence to learning and relating. We block the attempts those around us make to express their truths. We hurt others by withdrawing, attacking, or discounting their sense of reality and we mar our own ability to connect and learn how to relate better.

What gets in the way? Several things reinforce our old, failed models of defensiveness and prevent us from becoming more effective in dealing with criticism. They include:

- Past wounds
- Future projections
- Mistaking form for substance

Past Wounds

These come from experiences in your personal history where you felt hurt or damaged by the actions, inactions, or words of others. If these experiences were powerful enough initially, or if they were repeated, the equivalent of scar tissue formed on the psyche. This scar tissue is very sensitive to any stimulation that remotely resembles the past experience. As people confront us with their view of reality—especially if the confrontation is critical of us or our behavior—our scar tissue is often disturbed. We feel pain, are threatened, and automatically become defensive. These patterns, which we developed to help us deal with pain, are largely automatic processes that can take over unless we actively inhibit them and make conscious choices in the moment.

In Sally's case, her mother had come from a family with a verbally abusive father. She had deep scars from being told repeatedly that she wasn't "worth a damn." Elizabeth had thus developed powerful defenses of denial, rationalization, and counterattacks. Her defenses were activated any time those close to her offered criticism or challenged her assumptions. She ruled her family with tenacity, tolerating no confrontation from anyone. But Elizabeth's defenses, which served her well in childhood, were destroying her marriage and her relationship with her daughter.

Future Projections

This is our powerful imagination working against us where we imagine a painful future state and create images and story lines for events that may or may not happen. These projections are really flights of fantasy we engage in, making mountains out of molehills and disasters out of irritations. Sometimes when we allow our fantasies to run wild, we create in our minds scenes of pleasure and success. But more often, especially when we are threatened, we create scenes of pain and suffering where we imagine ourselves being hurt or taken advantage of.

These future projections create such vivid images of the way we are—or the way things ought to be—that we deflect feedback from others. We get so caught up in living out some future possibility that we do not hear the concerns of those in front of us. These images can be very appealing convincing us that everything will turn out great—if only we can make things go exactly our way. In these circumstances, we are likely to block out, resist, or even become hostile to any-one offering feedback that runs counter to our preconceptions.

When we escape into future fantasies or create cata-strophic images, we no longer hear or respond to the needs and concerns of others. We remove ourselves from the possi-bility of learning from feedback. We make ourselves unavail-able and, ironically, we fail to anticipate the real out-come. It takes courage to challenge these projections for, in the thick of it, they appear absolutely true.

Mistaking Form for Substance

It is easy to forget ourselves—to mistake symbols for reality. We love each image, whether it's a piece of jewelry, a company logo, or a sign of status. When we mistake these symbols for the real substance, we end up like the man who went to a five-star restaurant, read the menu, and, with his mouth watering, ate the menu. Then he complained about the dry and tasteless meal!

Every day, many of us figuratively eat the menu instead of the meal. When those around us do not confront or criticize us, we begin to feel secure that we have their support. In truth, all we've done is disconnect the warning lights. We "eat the menu" rather than the meal. But in human relationships, the "meal" of life is spiced with criticism and confrontation.

Over the years I have worked with many people suffering blocked or problematic relationships as they tried to work through challenging professional assignments, or as couples struggled to reconnect their relationships during difficult times. Frequently they believe that criticism and confrontation are signs of serious problems, or even of a failed relationship. Negative feedback and negative reactions to feedback are often taken as signs of the other person's "personality problem" or that something is just "wrong" between them.

In fact, criticism and confrontation indicate there is a relationship! Consider the times in which you struggled to reach a decision within your own mind. You probably did not storm off in anger at yourself in those instances. After all, your best interests are most easily negotiated with yourself. And we know that whenever we are in a relationship with another person for a significant length of time, we can expect to face criticism and confrontation.

To be in an on-going relationship is to experience a paradoxical state of challenge and harmony, comfort and discomfort, alienation and accommodation. A dynamic, shifting balance between these states is found in any vital relationship. In fact, such a balance is required in professional teamwork, as well as in loving, intimate relationships. The smooth flow between harmoniously connecting, working, and supporting each other is often disrupted by challenges, resistance, and confrontations, which are then rebalanced by accommodation, negotiation, and occasionally, letting go. Both sides need to participate in this dance of emotional states if the relationship is to be vital and effective.

When we expect this dynamic tension, understanding that it is part of any long-term relationship, we are better prepared to face these tensions when they occur, working with the other person(s) to learn and grow. Confrontations are opportunities for making breakthroughs in our own thinking, as well as in living and working with others. They can become creative moments in which intense and compressed learning can occur.

The COO of a billion-dollar, privately held business was attending the first day of our premiere three-day leadership training and had just received his 360 feedback gathered from the CEO, other members of the senior team, and his direct reports. He was furious. "This is bull!" he said. "They are attacking my integrity."

In fact, he had received very high scores in the major leadership categories of competency, relationship dynamics, passion, and six of the seven key acts of courage. The area where he had suffered a low score was in the dimension of integrity—the courage to be confronted. He was not a happy camper!

"I deserve better than this!" Face flushed and voice strained, he had clearly been hijacked by his limbic system— his emotional center. "They are telling me I am dishonest," he said. His interpretation was that they were telling him that he was untrustworthy.

Getting him to step back and look more objectively at the data was difficult. "Let's look at what they are really saying here. They are simply telling you that you get defensive when confronted with a perspective you don't like," I said.

"No, I am NOT defensive."

"That is defensive right there."

He retorted, "No, it is not!"

So we went, back and forth for about five or six more iterations before he suddenly laughed. "I guess I am sounding pretty damn defensive here."

He had reached a moment of realization—of openness—where he could see his behavior as others saw it. He realized that he did indeed come across as hostile to contrary viewpoints or perspectives.

"Your 360 data show that you have great skills as a leader. You are knowledgeable, have great expertise, are passionate about the business, caring about people, build good relationships, and have six key acts of courage in evidence. What you haven't had, up until this point in time, has been the courage to be confronted—to set your ego aside in service to your passion to help the organization be the best it can be. Your defensive response to critical feedback from your people damages your integrity."

He asked, "OK, but what does getting upset when I don't agree with someone have to do with my integrity?"

My answer was in the form of a question—so he would be able to take it in instead of deflecting it. "How do you feel about someone when you are giving them feedback about something you believe they need to see or do differently and in response they get defensive, won't listen, or deflect?"

"I don't like it," he said. "I get frustrated with them."

"Yes, and do you respect them more or less when they won't listen and start defending?"

"I respect them less," he said.

"OK, now how do you think others feel about you when you get defensive with them? Do they respect you more or less?"

He looked startled as realization occurred. "They respect me less," he sheepishly replied.

He was damaging his integrity and the respect others had for him due to lacking the courage to be confronted, to listen non-defensively. This was a breakthrough for him that empowered the next two days of the program. It led to a clear, actionable leadership development plan that leveraged his strengths and also laid out strategies and behavioral steps he would take to be even more powerful and effective as a senior leader. Follow-up in his organization demonstrated improvements in team functioning and the overall performance of the organization.

It is amazingly powerful when we are willing to be open to other perspectives and inputs. We end up being better informed and less likely to be blindsided by others and by life. It is much more effective to let confrontation in and respond openly, positively and courageously than it is to defend. Respect goes up internally, as well as externally. This allows us to respond more creatively, effectively, and wisely.

SUMMARY AND EXERCISES
Developing the Courage to Be Confronted

"...and as you sing, you are."

Your ability to learn from criticism and confrontation depends on your capacity to embrace it instead of relying on automatic defenses. This requires that you:

1. Understand that to be in a relationship is to face regular criticism and confrontation. This is part of the nature of "relating."

2. Develop a support network to help you respond without resorting to your automatic defenses. Whenever you do resort to them, have people around you who can compassionately help and encourage you to open up.

3. Give up the need to be "right." This means you need to develop your self-esteem and inner wisdom to the point where you know it is more important to learn to relate to others and to win than it is to be "right."

4. Realize that the criticism that most upsets you may be pointing directly to an area you need to address in order to learn and grow.

Here are some things you can do to create this courage and develop your capacity to let yourself be taught:

First: Resolve to learn from others when they criticize or confront you. The only barrier to learning is the scar tissue on our ego caused by old wounds, future projections, and mistaking form for substance.

- Notice what kinds of criticism or confrontation activate your automatic defenses. Are they triggered by criticism about your abilities, thoughts, appearance, actions, expressions, or your work? Does any type of confrontation and criticism disturb you?

- Look for the root of your defensive patterns. Once you see how you go on "automatic" and when, notice what you say to yourself, in either words or images, which feeds that defensive response.

Second: Resolve to embrace the criticisms and confrontations you receive. Remember, safety lies in being defenseless. You will always be more hurt by defending than by opening yourself up to feedback.

- Take each criticism and confrontation as an opportunity to be the student, to learn more about yourself and the workings of your own mind and heart—as well as those of others.

- Consider each confrontation as an opportunity to understand how the other person's mind and heart work and how they see the world. Seek to understand the other person better and, if you wish, build a stronger relationship.

Third: Seek out opportunities for receiving criticism and confrontation.

- Ask yourself, "What do I think needs defending? Is it worth the energy I am expending to defend it?"

- Ask others to engage with you in giving and receiving confrontational messages.

- Practice listening with your heart as well as your head. Learn to be suspicious of any automatic defenses you use.

- Create a network of relationships in which those around you are supportive, compassionate, and honest enough to help you "see" when you are getting trapped in automatic, pre-programmed ways of thinking, acting, and dealing with others.

- Notice any time you feel heavily invested in "being right" and engage in giving up the need to be right. Turn your attention to why you feel you need to be right and use this discovery to expand your mind and soul.

- Be gentle with yourself. When you feel most defensive, it is likely when you most need to be encouraging and kind with yourself. Use the defensive feeling as a tracking device to locate where you have been blocking your ability to learn. You will almost always find a fear behind the defense. Gently address this fear by remaining open and encouraging yourself.

"You thought you were the teacher,
and find you are the taught."

THE FIFTH ACT

THE COURAGE TO LEARN AND GROW

The courage to learn and grow is the commitment to challenge your assumptions—to slay your own sacred cows. It means moving from the certainty of what you know to the mist shrouded regions of ambiguity and doubt. It takes great courage to let go of what you have been, to step out of your comfort zone and seek new understandings, self-definitions, and ways of being and acting.

The courage to learn and grow is essentially the willingness to go beyond the first impulse that comes when you are challenged or in doubt. It requires the courage to face the unknown and the new. It means looking deeply into your heart and letting go of the need to be right and stay in control. It is found when we step into ambiguity and explore new territory that at first makes us uncomfortable. It opens the way to enhanced learning and more powerful and effective ways of relating to the world. As the visionary poet William Blake observed, "Knowledge is only the ratio of what is known. The ratio of what is known will change as we learn more." Einstein expressed it, "Imagination is more important than knowledge." To learn means to let go of the known and let our dream, our imagination guide us.

Dr. Chris Argyris has written extensively on how smart people stop learning because of their successful achievements. They get stuck in being "right" and remain heavily invested in the dead weight of what worked for them in the past. His studies show that we get stuck in behaviors that we believe contributed to our success. We become attached to—even rigid about—particular ways of thinking, acting, and interacting. This may be fine if the old patterns still fit and serve the changing world and work requirements effectively with their new processes, relation-ships, or roles. But when they don't—which is often the case—we experience loss and failure, often blaming others while we hold tightly to our cherished beliefs and behaviors.

My old mentor, Dr. James Noble Farr, understood this danger when he would warn senior executives and those of us on his staff of the terrible disease, "hardening of the catego-ries." When we get overly attached to our old success and ways of thinking we limit future success. Thus, some of the most intelligent and successful people, unless they are particularly vigilant, are apt to be the slowest learners. Their ability to learn is hampered by the baggage they carry as the "require-ments" of success, which they pin to past patterns. I compare this to driving a car while only looking in the rearview mirror.

What happens to individuals also happens to families, teams, and organizations. According to Andy Grove, retired CEO of Intel, "Only the paranoid survive." Just as an individual can become stuck in past behaviors, so can organizations. Grove and other successful leaders are keenly aware of the dangers of success due to complacency and the addiction people often find in doing things "the right way" because of that success.

We place ourselves in needless danger when we do not remain vigilantly aware of our need to grow and change, and when we don't allow ourselves to let go of behaviors that have led to success. We must see current reality and find the courage to learn and grow by stepping into new, untried, and possibly ambiguous situations. When we fail to exercise this act of courage, we begin down a slippery slope of complacency while riding the sled of unchallenged assumptions. This can be particularly dangerous when we wear a blindfold of denial.

Compounding this, we humans have two strong imperatives that impact our abilities to learn and grow: The first is to predict what is going to happen in our world, particularly in relation to things around us. The second drive is to control the results of the first imperative. Together, these demand a high level of certainty about what is "right" and about how we can control developments in our lives. If we are not careful, these needs—and the impulses that go with them—often result in an addiction to being "right."

This plays itself out in many ways. We resist views and ideas that threaten our picture of how things are. The compulsion is so strong that we may sabotage ourselves and damage the things that are most precious to us. Sadly, many of us, it would appear from behaviors, would rather be "right" than happy. We will often fight for our old ways of thinking instead of learning or exploring different ways of perceiving, acting, or relating to others. We become trapped in our need to be "right."

I have seen people sacrifice their families, careers, teams, and even whole organizations by arguing over who is right— all for the sake of not being wrong. They would rather be right than win! By being "right," they miss out on creating loving and enjoyable relationships.

This addiction begins when we mistake form for substance, as described in the preceding chapter. It is easy to mistake winning an argument or having others capitulate to our view as important, but we often do not notice when we have damaged relationships or traveled down a path that has less to offer. Many times, others allow us to be "right" and win the small battles, even as we lose larger and more vital issues that would have constituted major life victories.

Psychologists have studied this phenomenon in laboratory rats. The studies can shed some light on how the human mind works and offer suggestions about why we behave the way we do. In one interesting study, a rat is placed in a maze with at least three different paths, each ending in a different "den" or resting place. The scientist places something, such as a piece of cheese, in one of the dens and the rat is placed at the beginning of the maze and allowed to explore.

At first, the rat explores the maze slowly, but it soon becomes more eager. It goes down the first tunnel, finding nothing of interest. It then finds its way back and explores the next tunnel, and so forth, until by accident, it finds the path that leads to the cheese. The rat becomes excited and gets to eat some of the cheese. The scientist then promptly places the rat at the start of the maze. Each time, the rat moves faster in its explorations and its ability to locate the cheese. This process is repeated until the rat "knows" where the cheese is and finds it quickly every time.

At this point, the scientist places the cheese in a different den. The rat is no longer able to find the cheese. It spent a lot of time and energy to learn where the cheese was, and it was there every time, but now it's gone. So, from the rat's perspective, it should still be there! The rat will continue to seek the cheese in the same place for a short period of time before it begins to explore other paths in the maze until it ultimately finds the cheese in the new location.

I knew this process of rats in mazes but it was a breakthrough moment for me when I heard a trainer share the perspective, twenty years before *Who Moved My Cheese* by Spencer Johnson came out, that the main difference between rats and most humans is that rats will eventually get it through their small heads that the cheese must be somewhere else. They will explore other tunnels until they find the new location. Rats place very little importance on being "right;" they only want the cheese.

Humans, on the other hand, know the cheese is supposed to be there and will become self-righteous about this knowledge. They continue to insist that the cheese will eventually show up if only they can work harder, or faster, or use more money, or get more people to agree on where the cheese is supposed to be. After all, "It has always been here; it should be here, and it soon will be here!"

By insisting on being "right," we don't explore other paths and end up missing out on the real thing. We mistake the form of being "right" for the real experience of getting the "cheese"— what we really want, and what will sustain our hearts and feed our souls. The "cheese," in human terms, is being loving and loved by others, or a sense of accomplishment and personal mastery, or winning and getting ahead in life. It is getting what you really want as opposed to what you think you ought to have. It is the capacity to learn faster and better. It is increased self-confidence, personal enjoyment, and success.

The need to be right can urge us to continue to walk dead-end paths, getting the dregs of what once might have been, but knowing—By golly!—that we are right. We all do it at times, no matter how smart we are. Doing things we know from experience will not work, but by maintaining the fiction of being right, we somehow convince ourselves we are winning—even as satisfaction, love, and success slip through our hands.

In my bachelor days, my best friend and I went on a vacation to Jamaica. It was the first time either of us had experienced a tropical island and we thoroughly enjoyed it. On our return trip, we passed through the Atlanta airport. He had borrowed some money from me in Jamaica and we were settling accounts as we walked to our connecting flight.

I told him he owed me five dollars for a loan at one of the open-air markets. My friend, who tended to be generous with anything but money, argued. He said he didn't owe me five dollars; at most, it was only 50 cents. Usually I would have simply given in to avoid an argument. After all, it was only five dollars and the amount was not really important to me. But in that moment, I decided to stick by what I knew was right—he owed me five dollars. I was totally willing to let him keep it, but I wanted him to acknowledge I had given him the money.

He continued to argue and mentioned other transactions during the week. I had kept a tab of the transactions and began, with some anger, to review them with him. Surprised at my anger and tenacity, he became angry in return.

I was tired of hassling with my "best friend" about money issues; I was fighting for the principle of the matter and wanted him to acknowledge I was right. This time I was not going to simply accommodate his "neurotic pattern." My friend, on the other hand, was tired of feeling judged and fought back against my "self-righteousness." The conversation became increasingly unpleasant and heated.

As I delivered my loud sermon to his angry and rigid face, I paused; a deeper impulse within me stirred. I let it surface and was surprised at how much pain I was feeling. As I opened up to the pain, everything seemed changed in an instant. I felt my anger evaporate and tears welled up in my eyes. The pain felt like layers of frozen hurt, avalanching into grief. I looked at him and let the emotions flow as I spoke from my heart instead of my pride.

Even as I spoke softly, I felt gratitude for having released the burden I had been carrying. Along with this inner freedom came a deep feeling of aliveness.

"I can't believe a few dollars is more important to you than our friendship. You are more important to me than the money. What I really feel is that I don't matter much as a friend."

My friend's face changed the instant he heard the new tone in my voice. I noticed tears in his eyes as he listened. Then he spoke with sadness and hurt from his own heart. "I'm sorry you feel hurt. It's just that you had this old look on your face of being so much better than me, and you sounded so judgmental—like I was contemptible. That look and tone have hurt me many times."

I was completely receptive to his words and feelings. They resonated with mine and, at the same time, gave me information and an insight I never had before.

The new awareness washed over me so powerfully that I could not speak for a while. I saw how, over the years of my childhood, I had constructed a defense of "superior judgment" as a way of dealing with my father's anger and disapproval. And I saw that I'd actually had power over my father when I used it. Now I began to see how it must have injured and hurt him, even as it had hurt others—including my friend.

In the days that followed, I put this new awareness to use, noticing my face and tone of voice in ways I never had before. I could now tell when I was going on automatic defense, feeling my face assume an old aspect of judgment and condescension. The strange thing was that the facial movements and tone were familiar, as if I had been aware of them all along, but only now had my heart opened enough to really notice. It was a revelation of how powerfully the mind, driven by ego, can block out the obvious.

My own tone of voice began to convey a world of information to me and I saw how I used it occasionally to put others on the defensive to protect myself from threats. This meant I could now consciously change my behavior instead of defending it. I could share—or at least examine—the hurt and then respond in a way that was more loving and effective. I experienced a profound improvement in my friendships and, God be praised, also in my relationship with my father.

My life, which had felt good before, became much more rich and loving. I felt myself growing and learning at an accelerated rate. It was wonderful. All I had to do was let go of my need to be "right." It was as if a door that had been shut in my psyche was now opened, leading to a garden of beauty in which more loving and joyful relationships were blooming.

What had been required of me in the Atlanta airport was the courage to learn and grow, which, as it turns out, is also the courage to face the obvious. I had to:

1. Choose to learn in the moment.
2. Be curious, wishing to learn what the deeper impulse was.
3. Let go of what I "knew."
4. Let go of being "right."
5. Step into ambiguity.
6. Listen with an open heart.

These keys have helped me as well as my clients over the years find the courage to learn and grow. Perhaps the fundamental decision is that of choosing the path of heart versus that of personality and ego.

The path of heart is the way of living based on a commitment to being fully alive. Taking this journey is one of discovery, joy, self-expression, and an enhanced relationship with the world. This path brings out our deep, innate curiosity and opens the floodgates of compassion and enlarged perspectives on life and self. As the Stephen Mitchell translation of the *Tao Te Ching* says in one passage, "Consider the world as yourself, and you will fear nothing."

SUMMARY AND EXERCISES
Developing the Courage to Learn and Grow

"You thought you were the teacher,
and find you are the taught."

The courage to learn and grow requires being willing to suspend what we know and break our addiction to being "right." Without it, we block ourselves from the ability to learn gracefully and quickly. We get bogged down in defensive maneuvers, proving others wrong or spending great energy to maintain our positions and ways of thinking. This slows the learning process and makes us vulnerable to the deadly disease "hardening of the categories," which can be fatal in marriages, careers, or organizations that fail to learn and grow.

First: Make the commitment to face your fears of letting go of certainty and the need to be "right." Decide you will get more out of life by continuing to learn and grow, by lightening your load and setting down the heavy legacy of proving yourself right and resisting new views.

- Let go of expecting the world to conform to your expectations. Instead, meet the world where it is, observing and learning from what is so.

- Challenge yourself to look at the world from different perspectives and new assumptions.

- Notice whenever you go on "automatic" and start defending or arguing your opinions.

- Watch, over a period of several weeks, whenever you start feeling "righteous" or are expending your energy to prove yourself right.

Second: Commit to live from a more open learning approach. The following process will help:

- Choose to learn in the moment. Let the moment be your teacher and guide. Look at what is immediately before you, not at memories or rehearsed responses and behaviors.

- Be curious; seek what the deeper impulse might be. Look for what is moving deeply in your soul—not in the mechanics of your personality. Ask yourself, "What am I feeling at my core? What might others be feeling—if I can get beyond my initial interpretations?"

- Let go of what you think you "know." Certainty is like rigor mortis for the soul, as well as the mind. What if you have been wrong in the way you have put something together? What if there is a more loving and powerful way of seeing and understanding what is going on?

- Learn to treat your judgments with suspicion. See if you can use descriptive language or questioning to understand from a deeper and more powerful place. If you are successful, you will see at least three different options for responding to and dealing with a person or situation. You will be more open to interaction and will use your power more effectively.

- Step into ambiguity. Focus on the "shades of gray." Notice how often your thinking is automatic and computer-like: "right versus wrong," "black versus white," "yes versus no," "off versus on," and so forth. Don't be lost in digital thinking; step into the richer, wider range of the analog universe. Argue the other side of your position first. Then look to see if a third perspective can be found that encompasses the first two alternatives. Look for the integrative whole. What can you learn from this larger viewpoint?

- Listen with an open heart. Work to see the essential self—the heart of the person with whom you're dealing. Feel what they are feeling. Listen deeply to your heart and respond first by feeling, then by looking deep into your soul before responding.

"You thought you were the seeker,
and find you are the sought."

THE SIXTH ACT

THE COURAGE TO BE VULNERABLE, TO LOVE

The greatest gift you have to give is yourself. There is no substitute. Are you courageous enough to be loved by others for who you are, to be fully yourself? To be needed? To own the unique gifts you bring to your work, your family, and your life? Are you courageous enough to realize you are "the sought"?

The courage to be vulnerable—to care, to love—is essentially the willingness to be penetrated by life and the genuine needs of others. It is the great act of courage in which you open your eyes to the fact that you and your portfolio of gifts, talents, and unique way of being are what is ultimately sought by those around you.

We have all been hurt, at times, by those we love, someone we trusted, or by disappointments, mistakes, accidents, and personal attacks. We all know what it feels like to be taken advantage of, lose a loved one, or experience a broken heart. Still, the choice to remain vulnerable—to be open to love—

takes courage. This requires choosing the deepest part of our heart as the center, as our compass and guide, as we live our lives and do our work.

To make this choice to be fully open to life is to challenge our old patterns of protecting ourselves—our automatic and pre-recorded actions and responses to others. Fear and anger can block us. It takes courage to walk through those emotions and remain open and available to life and those around us. To live our lives wholeheartedly means to practice the courage of opening up, making ourselves present, listening and attending to the needs, weaknesses, gifts, and strengths of those with whom we live and work.

When I was in graduate school, my last internship was at the VA hospital in Durham, North Carolina. I was assigned to floor 4-B, thoracic and general surgery. Out of all the patients and families with whom I worked, one person in particular stands out. He was a veteran of World War II dying from esophageal cancer. He could no longer talk and his meals were given through a stomach tube, since nothing could pass the swollen, scarred remnants of his esophagus.

His wife, daughter, and the daughter's husband traveled more than three hours by car to see him each week, staying in town on weekends. He was emaciated and wasting away, slipping in and out of consciousness. I was moved by the love, longing, and intense grief expressed by the mother and her daughter. He, on the other hand, lay in the bed, holding their hands, nodding at them, and smiling or crying as they talked. His eyes were already seeing another world, but kindness and love poured from his eyes when he gazed at his family.

During the few short weeks I knew him, I saw him growing weaker every day. I was frightened by the prospect of witnessing his impending death, but I prayed for courage and felt I should be there to support him and his family. In the process, I came to love and admire them.

When he died, I was in the room, along with his wife and daughter. He had been lapsing in and out of consciousness for days, the conscious moments becoming increasingly brief and infrequent. The last time he opened his eyes, I was there as he lifted his finger and his wife took his hand and caressed it. She lifted it to her lips and kissed his hand with such tenderness that tears welled in my eyes. As she cried, her daughter reached over and took her parents' hands in hers. She kissed each hand and covered them with her hair as her tears flowed. I saw the man's eyes flutter and close for what would be the last time. His breathing became labored and rough. The attending nurse suggested they speak to him, saying he could probably still hear them. They hesitated and I added my encouragement that they tell him what they most wanted him to hear.

They told him simply, clearly, and with many tears how much they loved him and what a wonderful father and generous man he was. They asked him to remember them in heaven. He slip-ped deeper into unconsciousness and ten minutes later, he took his last breath. Before the nurse led them away minutes later, the man's wife held his hand, stretching out the contact, sliding her fingers reluctantly across his hand and then slowly, and with great tenderness, laying his hand on the bed. Covering her face with her hand, she was led away with her daughter's arms around her.

In the intensity of that moment, I watched as she struggled to let go of his hand. It was as if a bolt of lightning struck me—shattering my denial of death—I understood at a visceral level that all we ever love—all we ever have—will be taken from us by death. We pay a great price, indeed, for loving others and being open to pain. Yet I felt incredible gratitude and inspiration in that moment. I knew I would ultimately say goodbye to all I loved. With brilliant clarity, I felt how precious this moment was, not only for the mother and daughter but also for me.

I also knew at that moment in my life, had it been my father—also a veteran of World War II as well as Korea—lying on that bed dying, I would have been unable to express the gratitude and love I had just witnessed. I was nearly 29 years old and I had closed my heart, seeking to protect myself when it came to relating to my dad. In that moment, I knew I had the power to change the trajectory and pathway of that relationship.

These words came to mind unbidden: "Choose love and love completely. Have what you have, and be fully present."

I had witnessed the pain and the joy of being penetrated by love—of being really loved and of loving another person. I knew then that to love, with the awareness of inevitable loss, requires great courage. It struck me that every true act of love is an act of courage.

It is impossible to love—to really give or receive it—if we are not vulnerable. Our very attempts to protect ourselves from hurt—by defending, arguing, withdrawing, and otherwise restricting our expressions of love—block us from showing and receiving love. We cut ourselves off from matters of the heart and then feel powerful longings for connection and meaning in life. Our emotional defenses are driven by the healthy desire to protect ourselves from pain and loss. But these defenses imprison our hearts, shutting us off from that which nourishes us. Our very attempts to protect ourselves from hurt guarantee that we will experience more hurt.

A highly intelligent, graceful, and beautiful woman once came to me for therapy. Her husband adored her, her friends admired her, and she had been on a satisfying spiritual quest. But she had recently become stuck and felt emotionally blocked. What was worse, she realized she had never allowed herself to receive the admiration or love of others. She felt great loneliness and longing and a shroud of emptiness wrapped her aching heart.

As we worked, it became apparent that she had made the

decision, unconsciously, to not enjoy what she had. She would not allow herself to need anything or anyone. She kept herself apart from others, including her husband, to protect herself from feeling vulnerable. To her, this meant she could not be hurt because she was protecting her heart from being broken. If anything happened to someone she loved, she believed it would not hurt as badly. "Besides," she said as we uncovered the pattern, "what you won't let in can't hurt you!"

But the truth was that the very act of with-holding love meant she couldn't really enjoy what she had. By denying herself the joy of being open and loving with others, she felt great emptiness and loss. I asked her to imagine her deathbed and consider how she would feel about herself and her life if she continued this behavior.

She began to sob, feeling a sense of loss and loneliness. "Why, I never really 'had' what I had—I blew it! By protecting my heart, I walled myself off from those who were most important to me." It was as if she had been invited to a feast but only ate crumbs from the table, thinking she wouldn't feel quite so upset when the feast was gone. She was afraid of getting what she most wanted and then losing it or being disappointed by the consequences of indulging. In minimizing the possibility of pain, she was avoiding what she most wanted.

She understood intuitively the emotional cost she paid in guarding and protecting her heart. The protective behavior, created as a means of dealing with her over-critical mother and then amplified when her beloved grandfather died, had become a wall to keep her emotions inside. She had decided never to let herself be hurt again. Great courage was required for her to re-engage her life at the heart level—to allow love and feelings for others to return to the surface. I shared with her my story of being with the veteran and his family and it helped to crystallize her resolve. She generated that courage over the coming months as she took increasingly larger steps to open her heart.

What You Seek Also Seeks You

Here is a wonderful secret I have discovered through many powerful experiences in my life: What you are most deeply looking for in life is also, with great loyalty and dedication, seeking you. You are the sought! Love is seeking you just as you seek it. What you long for is coming to you, if you will only get yourself—your ego, personality, self-limiting beliefs and judgments—out of the way.

I first experienced this when I was working overseas. In 1973, I was a clerk for the High Commissioner of Refugees Office at the United Nations in Geneva, Switzerland. I was 23 years old and was amazed at the diversity and richness of the world and people around me. This experience contrasted sharply with the States, where we only seemed to hear news about our own nation and community and very little about the rest of the world. In Switzerland, the news covered the whole world, with only a very small portion dealing with the United States.

My daily routines, and even the way I defined myself, were disrupted by the European pace of life and the challenges of a different language and culture. As a result, I prayed and meditated more than usual. My dream life also became vivid and compelling, offering insights about my relation-ships with my family, myself, and the world around me.

I had been recording my dreams for several months, spending my first hour each morning either in prayerful meditation or working with the content of my dreams. Gradually, I began to feel a stillness—a sense of peace of heart—that I had rarely experienced. The world around me appeared more vibrant and colorful. When I went for my daily walks (also a new behavior), I felt the earth rising to support me. I noticed the living power of nature as I remembered experiencing it as a child. I would "see" the bark of a tree with deeper textures and color, "hear" the song of a bird in a richness and tone, and "feel" gentle breezes on my face—as well as a thousand other sensations I rarely noticed.

After I had been in Geneva for about six months, I woke up one morning from a dream in which I had been sobbing, feeling a tremendous longing. It was a dream of loss, of being left behind and feeling utterly alone and unloved. I felt a great ache in my heart that was over-whelming. But realizing the dream was a gift of my soul, I prayed for the courage to embrace the longing and fully experience it.

I closed my eyes and opened up to the pain and longing. At first the feelings intensified, but suddenly, the intensity subsided to a dull ache. I soon found my mind filled with thoughts of breakfast and all the tasks that needed to be accomplished that day. Finally I got up, dressed, ate breakfast, and went to work, where my mind was filled with all the duties to perform. Immersed in the morning's work, I completely forgot the painful loneliness. In fact, my boss, Madame Schule, had to remind me to take a lunch break.

As I walked toward the cafeteria, I "woke up" from the spell of work and suddenly felt disoriented and alone again, my mind in turmoil and my heart full of pain. I stopped near the doors and looked at the people, who came from many different cultures and nations, all wearing diverse manner of dress—some in saris, some in suits, others in turbans. As I stood there, I was blessed by grace, as if the hand of some angel had brushed my heart, and I was filled with an overflowing sense of love and a profound peace I had never felt before. Suddenly, everything seemed absolutely right and natural. I felt I knew each person completely and perfectly, even though several hundred people filled the room—many of whom I had never seen before. Nevertheless, I felt profound love for each person, knowing our lives were intimately connected. My heart was filled with joy, love, gratitude, and peace. My whole body vibrated with incredible energy.

I took a lunch tray and selected some soup and yogurt, overjoyed by the touch of the containers, the smell of the food, and the face of the cashier, who smiled pleasantly as I paid her. As I walked to a table, everyone seemed to look up, beaming with greetings and acknowledging my presence in some way, whether by nodding or speaking. They all smiled and seemed to drink in the same contact I felt. It was a play of love and joy to be in that room with all those wonderful and loving people.

The feeling lasted for about an hour. Then it slowly faded, leaving me for the rest of the day and evening with a sense of wonder and a profound feeling of gratitude. The experience changed my life, pointing me to a career of exploring the depths of the human heart. It also taught me that what I was seeking also sought me. The key was to slow down and be "caught"—to realize I was, indeed, "the sought."

As I have worked with individuals, families, executives, and organizations over the past three decades, I find that the greatest tragedy is the incredible loneliness and the longing most people feel for a deeper connection with life. They search for a more loving way of relating to their parents, children, spouses, or God. This longing is often expressed simply: "I want to spend more time and share more of my life with…." The desire to know you are important, known, and loved, and to know that those you love feel your love and appreciation, is ultimately what is important. We feel a great hunger for love and meaning, for a more profound experience of being alive. It takes courage to face this vulnerability and allow what we pursue to actually catch up with us.

In the Hasidic tradition, there is a story of a great rabbi who had many students. It came to pass that this rabbi was dying. His students kept vigil around his deathbed to feel the comfort of his presence, and perhaps hear his last words of wisdom. One day, his students were startled to hear him cry out in fear about his imminent meeting with God.

"But Master," said one student, "what do you have to fear? You have the wisdom of Solomon!"

Another student spoke up. "Yes, and you have the courage of David."

Yet another student added, "And you have the moral integrity of Moses."

The old rabbi looked up at them and said, "Listen, I'm not afraid God will ask me why I wasn't a Solomon, or a David, or a Moses. I'm afraid He will ask me why I wasn't fully myself!"

Similarly, Rabbi Harold Kushner, author of *When All You Ever Wanted Isn't Enough: The Search for a Life That Matters,* says that as he has sat with powerful executives who were on their deathbeds, not one of them in their last hours wished for more money, fame, or time to complete their projects. Instead, they expressed thoughts such as, "I wish I'd spent more time with my family," or "I wish I'd known my children better," or "I wish I'd taken the time to know who I am."

When I worked as a marital and family therapist, I used the *Diagnostic and Statistical Manual,* then in its second edition, which describes all the diagnostic categories of emotional distress, psychological disorders, and mental illness using consistent terminology and descriptions for the many problems and complaints people have. Each diagnosis is found on a continuum: from mild to moderate to severe. After years of providing therapy, I developed my own diagnosis that seemed to account for just about every category of distress. I labeled it "Chronic Lack of Self-Love." By labeling this as the foundational issue, I was able to have a powerful and helpful impact most of the time.

In the years since I developed that diagnostic classification I have worked with thousands of people—many of them executives—and the diagnosis seems even more universal and useful than I first suspected. Every situation I have addressed, whether it involved an individual, a family, or an organization, rested on the foundation of Chronic Lack of Self-Love usually in the mild to moderate range.

In one example, the CEO of a $200 million company faced ongoing conflicts with front-line employees because of the high turnover of senior managers. The organization seemed "spastic," with many starts and stops as new executives brought in fresh initiatives and management styles. The CEO thought the problem was that he could not get people to implement his strategic vision. He saw the turnover as a sad but reason-able problem since the company continued to grow in sales and profits.

But it became apparent that the CEO could not tolerate criticism and insisted on being "right." He wanted his direct reports to praise his ideas and then to improve upon and execute them effectively. He insisted on hiring bright, competent, and aggressive managers who had been successful in other organizations. These executives did not view their function as "rubber stamps" for his views. They expressed strong opinions and compelling insights backed with logical analysis.

In a Leadership Impact Study conducted by my company, we challenged the CEO and the other senior executives to consider what undesired results they helped to create, perhaps unconsciously, through their actions. The study, along with anonymous feedback from the people impacted by his behavior, served as a wake-up call for the CEO. He began to see what had been getting in the organization's way. He felt a strong need to prove himself—to measure up—that was driven by insecurity. And because of this need to prove himself, he had seen himself as the sole champion of the organization and had not made room for anyone else. Whenever he received critical feedback, he reacted as if he had been told he was wrong and his defense was to prove himself right and the other person wrong. He lacked three essential acts of courage: to be confronted, to learn and grow, to be vulnerable. Yet, the most critical one, the foundational act of courage was that of being vulnerable. This lack of emotional strength created a pattern that was destructive to his real intent. The core of this issue was a Chronic Lack of Self-Love at the moderate end of the spectrum.

Gradually the CEO improved, learning to make room for others and hear critical feedback. He learned to address his need for love and approval in more conscious and effective ways. He developed the courage to be vulnerable—to allow himself to feel the respect and approval others felt for him without questioning their loyalty when they challenged his ideas. The organization improved dramatically in performance, doubling profitability over the next 24 months and his leadership became more powerful as a result.

To let ourselves be vulnerable, to love and be loved, requires great courage. It means challenging self-limiting definitions, thoughts, feelings, and assumptions. We activate this courage by developing the first five acts of courage: dreaming, seeing current reality, confronting, being confronted, and learning and growing. Still, the courage to be vulnerable and to love is different. We must consciously choose to be open and available to life. Without vulnerability, we cannot experience true love, nor can we allow others to fully express their love.

I have been coaching, talking, consulting and writing about the need for the courage to be vulnerable for more than fifteen years now. More recently, Brene Brown, a sociologist, has delivered a TED Talk on the power of vulnerability. It is a brilliant and articulate talk that I highly recommend if you wish to dive more deeply into this essential, foundational act of courage.

Max DePree, retired CEO and chairman of the board at Herman Miller, expressed this well. When asked what he hoped to leave as his legacy, he said, "I want people to say of me, of us, that we were a gift to the spirit."

To be a gift to the spirit is to have the courage to be vulnerable, to love. To give this gift to our families, our organizations, and our society is to remember that, ultimately, what we seek is also seeking us. We are the sought. We have the power to choose, each moment of our lives, to act with courage and be more open and vulnerable. And our choices, moment by moment, shape us and affirm our presence in the world and the ways in which we relate to and connect with those around us.

SUMMARY AND EXERCISES
Developing the Courage to Be Vulnerable, to Love

"You thought you were the seeker,
and find you are the sought."

The courage to be vulnerable, to love, can be daunting. So many messages run counter to the concept of vulnerability: "Be strong," "Never give in," "Be independent," "Keep your guard up," "Play your cards close to the vest," "Don't appear weak or vulnerable," "Don't trust anyone," and so forth.

First: Choose love. Consciously choose to be vulnerable. Realize that the best defense lies in being defenseless. Let go of the need to defend yourself or your point of view. Instead, look deep into your heart and the hearts of others. Entertain and play with the thought, "What I am seeking is also seeking me."

- Practice letting go of judgment. To judge is to separate yourself from life and from others. Instead, learn to be curious, to inquire and seek deeper understanding.

- Remember your dream—what you most wish to create. Remind yourself of what you most deeply desire. Affirm that dream and choose it again out loud.

- Write out what you most want and what you would need in order to become open enough to obtain it. What do you need to let go of or surrender to gain what you most desire?

- Look deeply at those you live and work with, as well as those around you. Open yourself up to their gifts, talents, and abilities. They may help you in ways you had not considered.

- Consider the concept of "tough love." Accept no excuses for failure to achieve the results required for success, yet always maintain compassion in interacting with others. Care about the person, but be tough on goals and required results.

Second: Practice letting go. Mentally rehearse opening up. Share your heartfelt feelings with others. Look deeply into the hearts of those around you to sense their needs.

- Allow yourself to explore your deepest longing, loneliness, or sorrow. Find a picture of yourself as a little child that touches the longing or compassion within you for the person in the picture. Place the picture on the mirror in your bathroom. Look into the those eyes and notice what you feel. Offer your love and appreciation to that child. Speak out loud, saying, "I love you, and you deserve to be loved and appreciated. I will take care of you, cherish you, and help you grow and thrive."

- Grieve for what you have missed or never had. List these things and be specific. Focus particularly on key relationships in your childhood and teenage years. Write a letter to yourself to express the grief, sorrow, or regret you feel. Allow yourself to mourn the loss.

- Pray, meditate, write in a journal, and examine your dreams. Invite your dream life to inform you about your inner life. Open yourself up to guidance from the deeper reaches of your soul. Allow the loving images, dreams, and thoughts that come to blossom. Write them in your journal. Draw a picture or series of pictures. Create a collage of the images that capture your feelings. Place the collage in a prominent place in your home for a few weeks and then create a new one, noticing what has changed and come to life within you.

- Imagine you are the sought, the beloved; feel the world reaching out to you. See yourself taking the world in your arms. As you breathe in, feel the light and air rushing in to fill you. Notice how the ground supports you, how the world rises to meet and take care of you. Understand that you are the sought and that a living spirit seeks to fill you.

- Care for your heart. Imagine going to the center of your being. Explore seeing, at the center of your being, an image of what you most love. Breathe in and out, feeling into the connection with it. As you breathe into it, let it fill your heart. Open to the space around you. Feel your heart expanding. Breathe in and out from it, and allow the image to fill the space around you. Imagine as you breathe that your sense of being fills the entire building, penetrates the ground, and expands to the air above the building. See and feel the image of what you most deeply love. Feel your capacity to love expand. Open to the sense of the world filling your heart and then to the awareness of it containing the world. You are the sought, the beloved, the loving.

- Practice silently blessing the different people you meet during the day. Pay particular attention to those who are struggling, or people you normally would complain about. Send a silent blessing instead. Notice what happens to your inner feelings as you do this over several days.

- Commit to having the courage to be vulnerable, to love. Notice the choices you make each day and each moment: to be open and loving, or be protective and defensive.

"Sing a song of glory,
and you'll be that glory;
Naught are you but song,
and as you sing, you are."

THE SEVENTH ACT

THE COURAGE TO ACT

The courage to act is, ultimately, what the other six acts point to in your life. When it comes down to it, will you have the courage to act—to put yourself on the line? The courage to act is the willingness to place yourself in "harm's way." To act requires the courage to leave the safety of being a spectator and enter the arena. It demands of you the courage to commit yourself and your heart and enter into a profound relationship with life.

The courage to act drives the other six acts of courage. However, the other acts empower, sup-port, inform, and direct the courage to act. They enable us to take action with greater insight and thus wisdom. Without them, we act in a vacuum, answering only the insistent, automatic calls of our ego and our comfort zone. But without the power to act, we lack the ability to move.

"*Carpe diem*" ("Seize the day") is the motto of those who cultivate the courage to act. Courageous action requires a full commitment of time, energy, effort, and the willingness to risk your ego. Until we act on what we believe and know and express what is in our hearts, we merely observe life instead of living it. The courage to act, married to the other acts of courage, is the mark of wholehearted living, and it forms a profound relationship with the soul or essence of who we wish to become.

In the wonderful *Earthsea* trilogy by award-winning author Ursula K. LeGuin, a young wizard named Ged learns about the courage of facing his fears and taking meaningful action. In the first book, *A Wizard of Earthsea*, Ged uses his magic to call up a spirit of the dead. In doing so, he lets loose on the world a demon from a different dimension. The creature wounds him, but Ged's life is saved by a mentor, who dies in the process of driving the demon off. Ged sets out to find his place in life, bearing on his face and in his heart the scars from the dark night when he faced the demon.

Out in the world, the young wizard finds he is being stalked by the demon. He flees in terror, turning himself into a hawk and flying to the home of Ogion the Mage, a former mentor whom he asks for protection. Ogion listens to Ged's predicament and then tells him that the demon will eventually destroy him if he continues to run from it. The demon, he tells Ged, will only grow stronger by feeding on his fears. By running, the young wizard will only destroy himself. Ged argues that running is the only thing he can do, but Ogion encourages a confrontation and then goes to bed. The young wizard spends a sleepless night mulling the wisdom of his elder. The next morning, when Ogion awakens, he finds a message: "Master, I have gone hunting."

When Ged pursues the demon that has been hunting him, when he faces it, the creature turns and flees. Later, after chasing the demon through different lands, he corners it. As the two come together, Ged sees that the demon is an exact replica of himself. It is, in essence, his shadow side. He claims as aspect of himself that he had disowned, becoming both more whole as well as stronger in the process. Thus, by having the courage to act in spite of his fears, the young wizard becomes able to integrate a wilder, unknown part of himself and gains power and wisdom.

Facing what we fear—acting rather than reacting—demands courage. It requires the courage to act in spite of doubts, obstacles, fears, or past disappointments and failures. When this is married to the prior 6 acts, we can act with greater wisdom and deeper insight.

When my father retired from the military, he threw his heart into a real estate insurance business that hinged on financing from a wealthy executive he had recently met. Within six months, Dad created millions of dollars in profits for the company and generated several hundred thousand dollars in commissions for himself—more money than he'd made in the previous three years combined.

Although he was elated, the commission checks did not arrive as scheduled. He called the insurance underwriters, who assured him the checks would come shortly.

A few months later, as he sat at his desk, six men from the FBI came into his office. They escorted my father and two other employees into the conference room, where four additional agents surrounded the company president, whom I will call "Ron Gordon." The FBI had been monitoring Gordon and they had held up the checks from the underwriters.

A former insider to a mafia Don, Gordon had apparently stolen a substantial amount of money from his former associates. He changed his name to avoid detection and used the stolen money to set up a legitimate business. The FBI informed Gordon that there was a contract on his life. The business was closed down, having been started with stolen money, and all proceeds were held or confiscated. My father and the two employees were released, having done nothing wrong, but Gordon was placed in the Witness Protection Program. Everyone was to return home, forget about Gordon, and pick up their lives without contacting any company clients.

My father was shocked that the man he had trusted was not who he seemed and that all he thought he had earned was being taken away. As the FBI rummaged through his office, my father returned home, now facing the lowest point in his life. Eventually, Dad was allowed to see Gordon one more time, under agent supervision, to say good-bye. He asked his erstwhile "friend" why he had lied to him; Gordon answered that he simply wanted to start his life over with his family. He then apologized and the two men parted.

For three days, my father remained at home in his room. He seemed to have given up hope. Neither World War II, nor the Korean War, nor other losses or hard knocks had ever beaten him and his "can do" attitude. But one con man who had tried to go straight had apparently sunk the unsinkable. Dad appeared utterly defeated.

On the third day, he got up, looked at my mom, and said, "I don't know what will happen, but I can at least take action to make a new beginning." He went out and began to sell again. Over the next five years, he created a new company. He later told me that the love of his family was what allowed him to move forward in the face of betrayal, business failure, huge debts, and financial loss. He said, "I didn't want you to think it is okay to just give up. We all owe more to our families than the easy way out, even though sometimes it's tempting to just give up." He had found, once again, the courage to act. A lifetime of challenges enabled him to rise from his crushing disappointment and start over.

The courage to act is the willingness to commit yourself and move forward on what is in front of you instead of bewailing what was, or dreaming of what might have been. It is the bold, brazen act of stepping forward and seizing your life. It is taking the opportunity to create your life in the moment, regardless of what you face. It is moving towards your dreams and claiming your internal resources even in the face of fear and the specter of defeat or loss. What informs and assists in the most difficult of moments are the prior acts of courage that you have cultivated, bringing both resilience and guidance to your actions.

During the Battle of Gettysburg, the Army of the Potomac, over 100,000 strong, faced the 70,000-man Army of Northern Virginia. The Union army had suffered many defeats at the hands of General Robert E. Lee and his brilliant commanders, General "Stonewall" Jackson and General Longstreet. Newly appointed Union Commander General Meade held the high ground near the town of Gettysburg, while Colonel Joshua Lawrence Chamberlain held the flank position of the Union line.

On the first day of the battle, July 1, 1863, Confederate forces drove Union forces out of the town and seemed to prevail. On the second day, Lee intended to flank the entrenched Union Army by taking a small hill called "Little Round Top" where Colonel Chamberlain was positioned. Chamberlain was told he could not retreat; he was to hold the position to the last. During the long afternoon, Chamberlain's forces held their ground, repulsing multiple attacks by some of the best soldiers in the Confederacy under General Hood. By evening, Chamberlain's command had been reduced to less than 200 men and most were out of ammunition. The hard-pressed Union army had been unable to provide reinforcements or supplies.

According to Chamberlain's account, in his book *Bayonet! Forward: My Civil War Reminiscences*, as he looked down the sloping hill at the Confederate forces mounting yet another attack, he knew that if he stood his ground with little or no ammunition, his line would be overwhelmed and fail. He also realized that if he retreated, Confederate forces would sweep up the hill and outflank the Union army, which would then lose the battle and possibly the War.

He quickly sized up his options and selected the one plan that was most improbable—and also most direct. Stepping to the front, he shouted, "Bayonets!" His 200 men affixed their bayonets and followed him in a charge down the hill toward some 500 fully armed Confederate soldiers who were attacking his position. But the frenzied attack, and the surprise of Chamberlain's action, stunned the Confederate forces. Many of them turned to run and Chamberlain's small, poorly armed force saved the battle for the Union.

Certain defeat was turned into victory by Chamberlain's courage to act, which came both from conviction and the prior examination of his soul. He acted from self-awareness, practiced study, and confidence about what he and the Union army were doing, their mission to preserve the nation.

As I mentioned earlier, the courage to act is derived from the other six acts of courage. Without the first six acts, we ultimately have no sustainable capacity to take meaningful action. Yet, without the courage to take action, the other six acts remain fruitless.

1. The courage to dream and put forth that dream. My father and Colonel Chamberlain both had dreams about what they wanted to create and they put forth their dreams to all who would listen. Without the boldness of a dream—a larger purpose to our lives and work—we lack inspiration and direction.

2. The courage to see current reality. Both men suffered no illusions that their tasks would be easy; they saw current reality and the peril within it. They realized their resources had been spent, yet they still faced the stark options before them. Without the courage to see current reality, we remain unaware of what we face and what we have to work with, as well as ignorant of how to go about our work most effectively. Telling the truth to ourselves and others about where we stand, and about what we are standing for, is crucial in gaining the traction to move toward our goals.

3. The courage to confront. In each case the two leaders were willing to confront the people around them with the truth of the situation, and both confronted the situation itself. Without the courage to confront, we cannot assert ourselves in the world, nor can we claim our power. Instead, we live lives of partial paralysis as we resist expressing ourselves.

4. *The courage to be confronted.* The two men were willing to see what was facing them as well as hear the truth from others and avoid the pitfalls of wishful thinking or denial. If we do not listen to others or allow ourselves to be confronted by the truth, then we are at the mercy of forces we cannot see or acknowledge, vulnerable to failure, and blind to greater effectiveness.

5. *The courage to learn and grow.* Both were lifelong students of their chosen professions and of life itself. They studied, read, thought, and put into practice many new behaviors and ideas, stretching and preparing themselves to handle whatever challenges might come with courage and competence. When we lack the courage to learn and grow, to give up our addiction to being "right," we do not learn quickly or effectively—we do not adapt to new circumstances and we fall behind.

6. *The courage to be vulnerable, to love.* My experience with my Dad and my reading of a number of biographies about Chamberlain, particularly *Soul of the Lion: A Biography of General Joshua L. Chamberlain*, showed that each of them opened their hearts to the people with whom they worked and listened to their thoughts and feelings. They were sustained by the love and support they received and could inspire others by touching their hearts. When we do not allow ourselves to be vulnerable or feel the love and needs of those around us, we develop dry and brittle souls. We deprive those around us and ourselves of the greatest gift we have to give: Giving and receiving genuine appreciation, caring, and love.

7. *The courage to act.* Predisposed to act and prepared by a lifetime of countless small choices to deal with what was before them, my father and Colonel Chamberlain both were ready to act when crises and challenges arose. In fact, the small choices in acts of courage became significant ones, since the smaller acts prepared the men's minds and toned their hearts for the larger encounters. This act of courage is the defining act, since all acts of courage ultimately rest upon our willingness to take action and commit ourselves to a course. Without this act, we merely rehearse for life and never really live it.

What we act on and how we take action ultimately determine who we become in life. Our lives are woven from the day-to-day choices we make about the things we will and will not act upon. The courage to act means that whenever you sense a challenge in your life or work, you must move to understand and address it. Move toward the challenge, not away from it. Learning to move toward the challenges in your life is to cultivate the courage to act—as opposed to react. It is the choice to seize the moment, to seize the day. Through action, whether we are pursuing what we desire or addressing challenges before us, we shape ourselves as well as our lives. We become what we do as well as what we avoid doing.

All our acts of courage will come to nothing unless we have the courage to act on the truth as we see it and pursue what we most desire. This act of courage is developed through commitment, discipline, intimacy, and focus.

Mother Teresa, considered by many to have been a modern-day saint, was relentless in this particular act of courage. She had little regard for authority, titles, egos, the past, or excuses. She always found the courage to act in the moment and confront whatever was in front of her, occasionally deferring—only slightly—to the Pope. She was predisposed to act with integrity and full commitment, always speaking on behalf of the poorest of the poor.

Her whole life was based on courage, built by countless acts. She found the courage to leave her family and commit to being a nun. She had the courage to leave her country for her mission in an Indian convent. Then, responding to an even deeper call, she had the courage to leave the safety of the convent to live and work in the streets of Calcutta. Each act of courage developed her capacity to perform even greater acts. Her whole life was shaped by her courageous choices and actions.

The courage to act is the power we all have to shape our world by shaping ourselves. Each action—or inaction—helps form our conscious-ness, our future behavior and our lives. In fact, modern science indicates that the very biochemical processes that keep us alive are impacted by our thoughts and feelings, and thus by the choices we make.

In *Molecules of Emotion: The Science Behind Mind-Body Medicine*, Dr. Candace Pert, the re-searcher who discovered pheromones, also discovered neuropeptides, the molecules that influence our biochemical processes and our nervous system. Consequently, neuropeptides are closely connected to how we think and feel. Her research shows that whenever we have a thought, an emotion, or make a decision, our body pro-duces these molecules. These neuropeptides then act like keys, unlocking reactions in both the brain and the cells of the body, such as the immune system. Her research has led to a new medical science: psychoneuroimmunology.

Simply put, we become what we think, and how we indulge our thoughts as well as our feelings. More accurately, what we consistently think is what we eventually shape ourselves into being as well as accomplishing. Our choices—the thoughts and emotions we entertain—impact how our mind and body function, actually shaping them. What we choose to feel, think and act upon affects the chemistry of our brain and body. We have the power of choice: to act, think, feel, express ourselves, and interact in ways we see fit. This power not only requires courage, it requires knowledge and practice. It is not simply a matter of taking the "path of least resistance." The courage to act—to choose, to move beyond fears, doubts, comforts, old ways of thinking, and the resistance of others—is the pivotal act of courage that will allow us to live our lives wholeheartedly.

SUMMARY AND EXERCISES
The Courage to Act

"Sing a song of glory, and you'll be that glory;
Naught are you but song, and as you sing, you are."

The courage to act is the willingness to "sing our song of glory" and realize that "as we sing, we are." How we choose to "sing" determines who we are today and, increasingly, tomorrow. Each act shapes our lives. We live more wholeheartedly when we act with courage. It is through our acts of courage that we experience joy.

Prepare yourself to give traction to your dreams and aspirations. Great power may be found in seemingly small actions, such as writing down our commitments and dreams. Power is unleashed within our souls when we consciously choose our thoughts by directing them toward what we can do and what we would like to experience. There is also potent "magic" in using the imaginative power of our souls to create and apply helpful images in working with the deeper, nonverbal parts of who we are. We have the power to act courageously by simply using imagination—perhaps coupled with drawing, writing, or the spoken word—to shape our interior landscape as we prepare to act in the larger world of family, friends, organizations, and society.

First: Resolve to face yourself. Know that what you don't face today will continue to drive you and shape you into something you may regret. Resolve to move toward the conflict. Act by facing what frightens you, what you are resisting, and what you have historically stumbled over. Take the "tadpole" today over the large "toad" down the road that you will have to eventually "swallow."

- Look at the exercises from previous chapters, especially the courage to see current reality. Review your journal entries to look for patterns or themes that point to what trips you up.

- What do you most resist looking at in your own life? What internal "demons" (things you deny or don't want to see, conflicts or problems you face) are you running away from? What have you been avoiding or neglecting? A good clue can be found in things people say that irritate you. Notice your reactions to others. What irritates you or upsets you may indicate something below the surface of your ego.

- List two or three major issues—behaviors, recurring anxieties and fears, relationship conflicts at work or home, or other sources of pain—that impact your life.

- Resolve to "own" the patterns and act on the knowledge that the patterns are yours and within your power to change.

- See yourself as having the courage to act on your life, both personally and professionally, as well as on your attitudes and self-limiting beliefs that may be problematic or off purpose for who you are and what you wish to create.

Second: Remember that what you choose—every thought or decision—has consequences. This occurs not only at the social level, but also on the molecular level in your body, in its immune system and brain functions. What you think and choose shapes your biology and your unique human destiny.

- Review your journal to understand your thoughts, choices, and decisions. What would you change about how you have shaped your biology and your destiny? List the changes you would make.

- Make sure the list corresponds with what you most deeply desire and want to experience. (Review your dreams from the first chapter.) Select two or three of the most critical choices that would best move you toward your aspirations.

- Consciously choose the list. For example, "I choose to experience myself as loved and loving," or "I choose to face my fear of rejection by speaking my truth," or "I choose to express my love instead of holding it inside." Speak your choice out loud.

- Visualize yourself acting with courage in life. Create a collage or draw a picture of the ways you will be acting and living. Depict in images the choices you have made and will be making.

- Invite your soul to speak to you through dreams, inspiration, images from the natural world, or other synchronicity, such as in songs you hear or books that come into your hands, or a "chance" meeting or conversation. Choose to be receptive to inspiration and messages of guidance and encouragement along with other tools and resources. Choose to have a deeper and more intimate relationship with Creation and with your soul.

- See each day as a quest for developing your courage muscles and shaping your life and the world around you. Choose your deepest intention and remind yourself that you are shaping the rest of your life by every action and choice: by what you do and don't do, what you say and don't say, and what you think and dwell upon.

- Claim your life. Act on what you most want to create. Choose to act today from the center of who you are.

The Courage to Act

Sing a song of glory, and you'll be that glory;
Naught are you but song, and as you sing, you are.
You thought you were the teacher,
And find you are the taught;
You thought you were the seeker,
And find you are the sought.
Sing a song of glory, and you'll be that glory;
Naught are you but song, and as you sing, you are.

—SUFI CHANT

CONCLUSION

LIVING OUR LIVES WHOLEHEARTEDLY

The 7 Acts of Courage represent a larger unifying process of living our lives with integrity, meaning, and power. This complex process may best be understood by separating the distinct forms of courage required for living a whole-hearted life. We can shape a life in which joy is frequent by learning to discern which act of courage is required and then learning how to engage that act. We can develop our capacity to act wisely and courageously by first identifying which act is needed and then practicing that act both in our imagination and our lives.

I compare the 7 Acts of Courage to the seven cardinal directions held sacred by the Native American tribes. They provide orientation and direction on how to live full and wholehearted lives, regardless of the circumstances. They offer clear choices and actions to empower your life and observe and understand the world. They also point to where the powers to learn, grow, and act with wisdom and compassion in any situation may be found. To me, the seven sacred directions are more helpful and profound than our four points of the compass, which are based on a two-dimensional model. As Native American tribes realized, a more complete set of directions includes:

- North
- South
- East
- West
- Up
- Down
- Within

These directions, when applied to courage, are guides to a well-rounded and wholehearted way of life. They lead to a richer way of expressing your gifts to the world around you. Just as we need the four cardinal points of the map and the vertical dimension that includes up and down, we also need the dimension of the soul—within—if we are to live with mastery, depth, and fulfillment. In this setting, courage is appropriately applied to the seven cardinal points. Just as the seven directions offer guidance and direction to those who honor and follow them, so too the 7 Acts of Courage offer a profound means of orienting, guiding, and inspiring us.

North: The Courage to Dream and Put Forth That Dream

North has historically been the direction for orienting people on the earth to go "True North," just as the courage to dream and put forth that dream is our orientation and guidance to our own destiny. In Native American traditions, north is the direction of wisdom—the deep, guiding wisdom of our inner spirit that reminds us of our deepest aspirations.

A 67-year-old woman had a dream for herself. After she raised eight children, she decided she wanted to obtain a college degree and become a journalist. Her grown children tried to talk her out of this "fantasy," but she was stubborn. Over the next ten years, she took courses here and there and finally earned her degree at age 77. She landed a job writing political commentary for the local newspaper! Clearly, this woman had the courage to dream and put forth her dream to the world. She had the courage to orient herself and follow her star.

South: The Courage to See Current Reality

South is traditionally the direction of warmth, of touching the earth and being grounded. It is the opposite of North, which represents dreams. To the south is heat, or pressure, in opposition to the dream. It represents what stands in the way of our dreams, but it also represents the ground on which we stand.

A young mother of two felt depressed and overwhelmed. She shared her pain about the lack of love she felt from her husband and how distant he had become. He completely ignored her sexually and she was afraid of what it might mean. I asked if she could step back and be the compassionate, observing friend to herself in the situation, as she had been to so many others.

When she heard this, her mouth dropped open and she exclaimed, "He's having an affair and doesn't have the guts to tell me. He is lying to himself and me."

In that moment, she found the courage to see the truth she had been avoiding. She now saw her relationship with her husband in a new light. She engaged another act of courage by confronting him and, in the process, shaped a new life for her family. But she never would have been able to act if she had continued to avoid seeing current reality.

East: The Courage to Confront

East is the direction of illumination. It represents enlightenment through speaking up and confronting the people and situations you face. It is the direction of the sunrise, casting light on your own self-expression. Confrontation can be brilliant. "Sparks fly and they illuminate not only the people or situations we confront, but the soul itself.

Not too long ago, in what was at that time "Apartheid" America, a woman climbed onto a bus and sat in an empty seat near the front. She was told to move to the back where her "kind" be-longed. But her feet were sore and she was tired of the discrimination and prejudice. She was fed up with injustice.

Rosa Parks made history, finding in herself the courage to confront the tyranny of prejudice and racism through the simple act of sitting where she wanted to, rather than at the back of the bus—where people of color had been relegated. She proved to be one of the most visible courageous sparks in the civil rights movement. Her courage to confront a corrupt system and social order based on prejudice and intimidation came from the depths of who she was and the inspiration of leaders such as Reverend Martin Luther King, Jr. She challenged the status quo, enduring ridicule and threats in the process.

West: The Courage to Be Confronted

West is the direction of reflection and introspection. It represents the willingness to be confronted, to reflect on what comes to you as judgments, criticisms, and confrontations. In the heart, we either allow ourselves to hear others and their messages, or we get lost in the labyrinth of our own thoughts.

I witnessed an angry executive who stood up in one of our seminars, struggling with his anger. He had played professional football and still showed great physical power. He towered over the woman who was facilitating at the moment and who had just told him that his anger was damaging his life. "I don't have to listen to this!" he said loudly.

She faced him and undaunted and calmly, quietly replied, "No, you don't need to listen. You can turn a deaf ear if you want. Only you, and those who live with you, still have to pay the price. Do you really want me to shut up?"

The big man grimaced, but found the courage to ask, "What do you mean? What 'price'?"

The facilitator met his gaze and gently asked, "What about peace? Does your anger leave a wake in your life that is less than peaceful? Does it hurt you and those around you?"

The man visibly slumped as her kind tone penetrated his heart. "Yeah, I pay a price," he said. "I don't like the way I yell at my kids. It's hard to relax. In fact…" He paused and looked at her with pain in his eyes. "I don't enjoy my life very much."

Then he took the next step, which moved him deeper into the courage to be confronted. "Tell me what you see," he invited her. "I want to know how to break this pattern of rage."

He was courageous enough to examine how he had constructed his defenses. He was open to seeing how his anger toward his father, who left him and his mother when he was only 11, had contaminated his whole life. Despite his success in football and business, he was not able to enjoy it and seemed perpetually irritated or angry with people around him. Over the next few days, he considered his life and the choices he had made that were less than fulfilling.

On the last day of the seminar, he came into the classroom radiating energy. "I just talked to my father last night for the first time in over twenty-five years," he said. "He was glad to hear from me. I told him I wanted to get to know him and for him to get to know me before it was too late. It's like some huge grinding-wheel inside my gut has finally stopped."

By having the courage to be confronted, this giant of a man stepped out of the constricted heart space he had created and, for the first time, stood up to his full spiritual height.

Up: The Courage to Learn and Grow

Up is the direction we grow, toward the light. It is a symbol of higher power, spirituality, and growth. It represents learning about ourselves, about life, and about how to live life, as well as the courage to be students again. It means letting go of the hard casing of what is known—like a seed— and opening up to new possibilities and growth.

My grandmother, Marcie Haynes, felt completely overwhelmed. Her husband had become completely bedridden, slowly dying from diabetes. She still had five children at home to support, the last a pre-teenager. She felt the weight of caring for her beloved spouse while she raised the children and, somehow, earned a living.

Marcie had been through trials and challenges before. She was married at the age of 14 to a man in his 30s and she had seven children by him before she was 30. Her husband abandoned the family and she supported herself and the children working as a housekeeper. Then, later, she met and married a man who touched her heart and they had three more children. They loved each other deeply. Now she watched him—bedridden, sick, and wasting away. Despite her pain and breaking heart, she still had the rest of the family to support. She sought his help on how to care for the family's needs. She needed a job that would bring more income that would allow her to spend time with her husband and the three youngest children.

"Marcie, my love," Grandfather said, "you love children. You have a knack for calming people down. Why not become a midwife and help bring new lives into the world?"

She shuddered and debated with him out of fear. She objected that she didn't know enough, that she hadn't finished school, that she might hurt someone, that she didn't have the ability, and that she wasn't smart enough.

After she ran down a bit, he smiled. "Funny thing—you've helped deliver three children for other people, and one of them you delivered before the doctor even arrived. All he did was wave his hands and pronounce it a healthy baby."

As she started to object again, he interrupted. "Besides, you've had ten children of your own. That makes you a 'certified expert' on the subject. If you could do that, you can do anything."

She found the courage to study with a mid-wife and soon overcame the fear that she wasn't smart enough. In the following years, my grand-mother delivered over 300 babies, all healthy except for one stillbirth. She also supported her family and cared for her husband. My grand-mother showed the courage to learn and grow, moving into the world as a midwife and provider for her family.

Down: The Courage to Be Vulnerable, to Love

Down is the direction of humility, of planting and digging, and of putting down roots. It represents the vitality of what sustains us. It is where we penetrate the surface of our being and realize that what we most desire—what we most seek—also seeks us. We are the sought.

A colleague of mine, a gifted consultant and trainer, had just returned from an out-of-town business trip. It was Halloween, and as she drove up to her house, the neighborhood was filled with parents and children in costumes. She had no candy and believed Halloween was a nuisance, wanting no part of it. She put her car in the garage and slipped into the house, lighting only a candle and hoping no one would come to the door.

She was irritated with the world and herself for slinking about her house in the dark. Children rang the doorbell several times while she remained still, trying not to make a sound. But finally, after the fourth ring, she turned the lights on and answered the door, ready to admit she was home. She saw a little girl dressed as a fairy and a little boy dressed as a monster.

"I'm very sorry," she explained. "I just got home from a trip and I don't have any candy." She waited for the confrontation—or anger or disappointment in their faces. "That's okay. I can help you." The little girl reached into her bag and lifted out three big handfuls of candy, giving them to her. "Now you have lots of candy to give other children," she said.

"You really are a fairy godmother, aren't you?" marveled my friend.

The little girl beamed and replied, "Yes, I am." And the two turned and marched off.

My friend found the courage to be vulnerable. She spoke from her vulnerability and found an incredible gift of love flowing back to her. She felt she had become the sought, receiving love and a lesson in generosity from a little "fairy godmother" just when she needed it.

Within: The Courage to Act

Within is the direction of the soul and of mystery, of depth and personal mastery. It represents the inner wisdom to know when and how to act, to have the courage to act as needed in small, everyday matters as well as in large, life-changing events. It also represents the essence of who we are, moving into the world with authority and power even when we feel scared and doubtful. For in the act itself, we transcend our fears, doubts, egos, and personal limitations.

My father was stationed in Korea on a second tour of duty after the end of the conflict. One evening just after midnight, he awoke in his tent to the sound of rushing water and pouring rain. He sat up and looked at his watch.

It took him a moment to realize he was hearing another sound above the wind, rain, and rushing water: the sound of children screaming.

He rolled out of his cot and rushed into the rain. In his sleepiness, he thought his children were screaming, but the cold rain hit him with a start and he realized the screams came from a village near the small hill where his unit was camped. As he walked to the edge of the hill, the roar became louder and he saw a dark, rushing torrent of water smashing through what had been the center of the village. He ran back toward the camp, calling to the other men in the company. Flashlights came on and sleepy men made their way to the side of the hill. Their flashlights revealed adults and children clinging to poles—formerly huts—in the middle of the rushing water. Other families stood on shaking roofs half covered by water. A few adults and children had reached higher ground and were shouting to the people in the water, and then to the soldiers when they saw the flashlights.

My father, dragging every bit of rope he could find, came rushing back. He began frantically tying knots in the ropes. A number of others helped, tying lengths together. My father, terrified for the safety of the children, issued orders. Some argued with him above the noise, shouting things like, "There's nothing we can do!" "You can't order us to commit suicide!" "It's impossible to help them. Let's call for help!"

My father looked at the men helping with the ropes and

then at the others. He stepped closer and said, "I can hear the voices of my own children crying and they sound the same. Can't you hear? What if they were your children? Your wives? Will you help me?" All of the men participated in the rescue and many in the village were saved.

Consider the stories and examples in this book as well as the stories in your own life that have touched you, shaped you, and guided you. They are living illustrations of courage, pointing to something larger and more enlivening in our souls. Whether the acts are large or small, they predispose us to act with even more courage later on. We develop our "courage quotient index"—our CQI, the muscle of heart—every time we face our fears, doubts, or anxieties and act with integrity. Collectively, the 7 Acts of Courage form a tapestry that reveals the living spirit in our lives and helps us embrace a more wholehearted and joyful way of living and being in the world.

Personally, I am uplifted and amazed when I reflect on who we are. Each of us is a vast mystery. No one except the Divine can encompass—let alone comprehend—our true nature. Ultimately, we are unknowable, continually unfolding our mystery every day of our lives. The creative intelligence in our minds is awesome. We are a vital part of the universe and our actions—words and deeds—make a difference. It really matters what we think, and our thoughts impact the world around us. At the very least, the ways we think, the concepts we indulge, shape our attitudes, beliefs, and feelings, which in turn shape our actions, words, and lives.

Earl Nightingale states that the thought that shaped and liberated his life was a sentence he discovered when he was in 20s: "As you think, so you are." (*The Strangest Secret*) I would add the theme of this book: "Sing a song of glory, and you'll be that glory." The truth is, "As you act, so you become." Our acts of courage, then, shape our relationships and the world around us.

May we live each day of our lives with the courage to live wholeheartedly and thus create success, significance, fulfillment, joy, and love as our living experience and greatest legacy.

About the Author

 Robert E. "Dusty" Staub II is President and founded Staub Leadership International. He has spent more than 30 years working with individuals, organizations, families, and community groups to deliver effective coaching in personal and organizational leadership development. In the past 35 years, thousands of executives have gone through his intensive Helping Individuals Lead Successfully (HILS) seminar. Dusty is the author of *The Heart of Leadership:12 Practices of Courageous Leaders, Courage in the Valley of Death,* and co-author with Wayne Gerber of *Dynamic Focus: Creating Significance and Breaking the Spells of Limitation.* His material has been published or cited in many national publications, including *Fortune, Reader's Digest, Executive Excellence, The Business Journal,* and *LeaderQuest.*

Dusty is married to Dr. Christine Staub, a family medicine practitioner. The couple resides in Kernersville, North Carolina, with three adult children out in the world: Sean, Kendra, and Chamberlain. Dusty's interests include reading anything and everything, spending time with family and friends, taking long walks in the woods, sitting by an open fire outside and a life-time of practice in yoga.

Contact Dusty via e-mail:
dusty@staubleadership.com
Or call (336) 441–5344

About Staub Leadership International

Staub Leadership International is a comprehensive leadership development organization dedicated to helping its clients achieve personal and organizational effectiveness through improved leadership, empowerment, communication, and team-based creativity. The firm's unique approach combines elements of behavioral science with business-based practices to provide enduring solutions. The company partners with organizations across the spectrum of US industry, ranging from Fortune 500 companies to mid-size and small companies, helping their partners master the challenges of leadership and achieve bottom-line results.

Standard Programs

- Helping Individuals Lead Successfully (HILS)
- Sociomapping for Teams and Organizations
- Advanced Leadership Program
- Leadership Intensive Training (LIT) on-site with organizations
- Strategic Leadership Life Plan

Customized Packages

- Team-Based Creativity
- Team Development
- Leadership Development
- Individual Executive Coaching
- Climate / Organizational Studies
- Facilitation Training
- Leadership Intensive Trainings
- 360-Degree Assessments
- Keynote Speeches

The company offers a wide array of customized and tailored packages and processes that can benefit you, your team, or your organization.

For more information about our products and programs from Staub Leadership International, please contact:

Staub Leadership International
PO Box 876
Oak Ridge, NC 27310
Phone: (336) 441–5344
Fax: (336) 441–5336

www.staubleadership.com

Books by the same author

The Heart of Leadership
by Robert E. Staub II

Robert "Dusty" Staub tells us that those who purport to lead often fail because they don't understand who it is they're trying to be; they don't know how to lead. Dusty teaches us about the four chambers that make up the heart of a true leader: competency, intimacy, integrity, and passion, all in service to purpose (orientation) and a vision for moving forward.

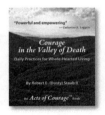

Courage in the Valley of Death
by Robert E. Staub II

Courage in the Valley of Death is based on a powerful life experience that led to the author's personal transformation. With just a few lines per page, this book serves both as an inspiration and as a practical guide to living with greater courage, grace and joy.